MW00653373

True Fellowship

Church as Community

by
Art Katz

BURNING BUSH PRESS
BEMIDJI, MINNESOTA, USA

True Fellowship: *Church as Community*
by Art Katz

First Edition:
© 2003 by Arthur Katz under ISBN 981-04-5462-7

Second edition, 2009

ISBN 10 digit: 0-9749631-6-X
ISBN 13 digit: 978-0-9749631-6-7

These and other materials of a comparable kind can be found at: www.artkatzministries.org

Published by Burning Bush Press

About The Author

Art Katz was born in Brooklyn, New York, of Jewish
parents, and raised during the Great Depression and
turbulence of World War II. Dropping out of high school,
Art became a merchant seaman, and was later drafted into
the Army and stationed in post-war Germany. He later
taught at an Oakland high school. Shattered by the
disillusionment and horror of the Holocaust perpetrated
against his Jewish kinsmen, Art embraced Marxist and
existentialist ideologies as the solution to the vexing human
predicament.

Hitchhiking through Europe and the Middle East while on a
leave-of-absence from the teaching profession, the cynical
and unbelieving atheist, anti-religionist and anti-Christian,
was radically apprehended by a God who was actively
seeking him. The actual journal of that experience, *Ben
Israel – Odyssey of a Modern Jew*, recounts Art's quest for
the true meaning to life, which climaxed significantly and
symbolically in Jerusalem.

Art attended Santa Monica City College, UCLA, and the
University of California at Berkeley, earning Bachelor's and
Master's degrees in history, as well as a Master's degree in
theology at Luther Seminary, St. Paul, Minnesota. With his
speaking ministry spanning nearly forty years, Art sought to
bring the radical relevance of the Bible's message to
contemporary societies, both secular and religious. With
several of his books translated into major foreign languages,
Art traveled frequently and widely as a conference speaker
and prophetic voice for the Church until his death in 2007.

Acknowledgments

The presence of a divine reality in the earth is surely one of the great cries of our times. In His wisdom, God intends that this reality be formed and fashioned in a corporate expression of His people, who desire and scck for the glory of this reality through a divinely ordained relatedness that can best be described as true fellowship. The contents of this book is by no means an exhaustive attempt to describe that reality, but it will, in measure, allow the reader to be apprehended by some of the essential elements that God is seeking to establish in the life of His people.

Little or nothing is mentioned on the subjects of church structure and government. Others have written more adequately on such themes, but few have attempted to probe and explore Paul's words: "To Him be the glory in the church."

The material for the book was compiled and edited from Art's spoken messages on the subject of fellowship, given at different times and places during his ministry years. Special thanks to Jeannie Clink, Thomas Lei and Bryan Purtle for their needful help and watchful editing skills in the final proofing, to Linda Dunaway for her careful transcribing of many of the audio tapes, and to Chuck Schmitt for the cover design.

Simon Hensman
Laporte, MN
April, 2009

True Fellowship

Church as Community

TABLE OF CONTENTS

TRUE FELLOWSHIP

Author's Preface

> Behold, how good and how pleasant it is for
> brothers to dwell together in unity! It is like
> the precious oil upon the head, coming
> down upon the beard, even Aaron's beard,
> coming down upon the edges of his robes.
> It is like the dew of Hermon, coming down
> upon the mountains of Zion; for there the
> Lord commanded the blessing—life
> forever.[1]

Dwelling together is much more than coming together for meetings; it is a daily relationship, an integration of life with the brethren in which we share the awareness of our imperfections and struggles in the faith. In the midst of that dynamic of life, God has commanded the blessing of the glory of His life. After thirty years of community living, I know that this is not an easy reality to obtain. There is a necessary redemptive suffering that is intrinsic to dwelling together, and makes that dwelling possible; it is called the cross.

In the final analysis, every issue in the walk of faith is the issue of the cross as the experience of suffering. Humiliation is a suffering, and when God called us to establish a community, I knew that I knew that I knew: "You have had it, Katz. This is going to be for you humiliation and suffering. You are going to

---

[1] Psalm 133

be found out. You are going to be living closely and intensively with other people on a daily basis in which your defects, your shortcomings, your sins and your failures will be revealed." But out of that matrix of life, the possibility of a reality was able to break forth that can best be described as true fellowship.

May these pages communicate to the reader something of that reality, and particularly the glory of that reality. And may we, with the apostle Paul, be able to say in our deepest hearts, "to Him be the glory in the church and in Christ Jesus to all generations forever and ever. Amen."[2]

Art Katz

---

[2] Ephesians 3:21

Introduction

From the inception of my salvation, and into the first four or five years of it, I intuited that something was wrong in contemporary church life. Where was the power of God? Where was the glory? Where was the apostolic reality? Where was the "kingdom come"? Why could we not say in our generation as the saints of old said in theirs: "Repent, for the kingdom of heaven is at hand"? Why were we trying to induce people to "accept Jesus" on the basis of the benefit that would come to them for accepting Him? Why were we not speaking to them in the context of a soon-coming King as Judge over His kingdom? Could it be that there was no actual kingdom at hand being made visible before them that would have given us the authority to press that issue?

The Lord's reply was to bring us to Minnesota, to a property that had previously been a Boys' Camp. When I stepped over the link chain that hung across the entrance to the property, the Lord spoke four things into my spirit: "Dominion. End-time teaching center. Community. Refuge." It was the beginning of a revelation of His kingdom that had its outworking in hardship, anguish of soul, and the terrible disappointments and frustrations that can only come to us in *true* church experience. I marvel at the naiveté of Christians who think that church is a place where they are going to be mollified or coddled. When rightly understood, church life is the very place in which God, in His wisdom, has reserved His most exquisite forms of redemptive suffering in order to bring us more rightly into the knowledge of Him and His purposes. That has been my experience, and I would not trade it for anything.

The church is called to be the "pillar and support of the truth."[1] To think that we can come to this character with others on the basis of a Sunday service and mid-week Bible study is to completely fall short of God's intention for the church. To come to this reality is going to take a people who recognize that church is not established for *our* enjoyment, but for *His* glory, and that it is an all-consuming, total requirement for which our jobs and careers are but secondary enablements.

We all suffer from an inadequate view of the church. We have allowed the world to relegate the church to a Sunday afterthought, a kind of Christian cultural requirement that somehow serves the purposes of those who might obtain some benefit from it. The world does not see church life as any more important than many other institutions that serve the purposes of mankind. Therefore, we need to have our understanding opened to an apostolic way of considering what the church should be in the purposes of God.

Most fellowships of today are essentially an aggregate of individualities; we sit alongside each

---

[1] 1 Timothy 3:15f

other, but we are not yet together in the biblical sense of that word. We do not yet constitute that wholeness or completeness. We do not yet reflect the genius of the unity that is in the Godhead itself, where the Son does everything for the Father, likewise the Spirit for the Son, and the three are One. When we come to that kind of corporate unity of deferring one to another, the principalities and powers of the air will know it; but God first needs to reveal to us how deep-seated our individualism, self-will and rebellion are.

The powers of the air captivate the souls of men, rooting them in time, and blocking from their consideration the things that are eternal. We cannot come to freedom from this evil influence by ourselves alone. Separation from the world is a painful process, and those evil powers are pervasive and strong. It is only through the support, the encouragement, the prayer, the wisdom, the counsel of others and the atmosphere that we generate together as the community of God's people that we can live and maintain that freedom without being sucked back into the power of the world. The provision of a closely-knit body of believers is one of God's principal means to enable His people to overcome those powers. The sons and daughters of God are those who overcome the world, the flesh and the devil, and there is no place more conducive for being or becoming this kind of people *except* in such an intensive setting.

There is not a living soul whose life is totally free from deception. Our lives need to be submitted to the examination of God through the brethren in Christ. It will be a painful revelation, but rather the pain now than the unspeakable pain of learning at the judgment seat of Christ that we were living a delusion. We may have thought ourselves to be spiritual, while all along we were far removed from the spiritual authenticity and reality we assumed we had. The Lord is not going to indulge our romantic or wistful view of what we think true spirituality is. His gracious provision is an environment in which the true condition of our hearts, and the things that would not otherwise have been recognized, have the greatest possibility of being revealed to us.

The quality of our fellowship with the Lord vertically cannot be any better or more authentic than our fellowship with the brethren horizontally. We cannot have the one independent of the other, and we cannot have the one out of proportion to the other. How many of us think that we can, and love to be solitary and isolated saints, having some kind of imagined and euphoric relationship with God privately, but hardly having any patience at all for the believers who make up His Body? How can we cherish the Head more than the Body, and how can we honor the Head outside of the Body? It is like the vertical and horizontal beams of the same cross, and the one is in exact proportion to the other, thus saving us from exactly that soulish thing we would love to indulge, namely, isolation, separateness and privatistic living.

God has called us to the fellowship of Himself, to the fellowship of His sufferings and to the fellowship of believers, and we are not going to see great grace and authority if we are not authentically related in the Body and with the Head. In other words, we cannot have true vertical relationship with the resurrected and ascended Lord independent of an actual and existential one horizontally in His Body.

The way our typical Sunday services are constituted serves a purpose and suffices to a certain degree, but falls short of serving the ultimate purposes of God, and it is these purposes that I want to contend for. As the conditions of the world become more extreme and polarized, people are going to be forced to choose more radically *for* or *against* God. We are in that painful interim between a conventional Christendom and the apostolic entity that God is wanting established again.

Chapter 1

Church as Community

In order to adequately fulfill the magnitude of end-time demands, God's people are going to be called upon to exhibit a quality of character beyond what we presently know in our comfortable, cultural and conventional Christianity. This brings to the forefront of our consideration the issue of a matrix of intensive life together as a mode of present living. Whether it is actual living communally on the same property, or living in close proximity, neither of these are to be thought of as ends in themselves, but rather as a means to a larger end, namely: "To Him be the glory in the church."[1]   Paul lets that statement stand without any explanation as to how that glory is going to be obtained, but leaves it for *us* to search out the meaning and make the application.

We need to consider becoming a community in the sense of a closely-knit integration of a shared life

---

[1] See Ephesians 3:20-21

together. If a group exceeds the numbers by which intensity and truth of relationship are feasible, then it cannot, in my opinion, attain to true fellowship. A generalized congregation of three hundred, five hundred or a thousand cannot achieve what I am suggesting. Sadly, large membership is the great emphasis today, and constitutes a moving away from God's very provision for our ongoing sanity and sanctification.

Through years of intensive community experience, I have gained a view of church that has revised my understanding of the meaning of that word. In our time, church has become a misnomer, not just in fundamental and evangelical Christianity, but even in the finest forms of Pentecostal and Charismatic life. If our whole church experience is confined essentially to a Sunday service and Wednesday evening bible study, then it has become a caricature and distortion of God's original intention. If we have come to measure the success of a fellowship by how much we like the services: whether they are pleasant, whether the music is enjoyable, whether the preaching is good and how good the programs are, then we already have a faulty view of the church. However much *we* may applaud any of these aspects of a service, we need to understand that that very standard of measure is the indication of how far we have departed from the Lord's understanding of the *glory* of the church. We can conduct superb styles of Christian church services by accommodating the desires and tastes of our congregations, but we will never demonstrate the kingdom of God on that basis.

Church as community suggests a band of souls sharing a common pattern of life and spirit, seeking as their first motive the manifestation of God's glory in the earth through the relationships established in the intensity of daily life together. When we established the beginnings of a community in northern Minnesota, we hardly knew what church as community meant. In the anguish and enormous humiliations, and in the terrible defeats and failures of all of our pet evangelical convictions, which burst like a bubble in the reality of the demands of an intensive life, something began to dawn on us. Though we did not understand it at first, we caught a glimpse of some of the essential elements that allow for the glory of God in our midst.

I am an enemy of any kind of utopian or social experimentation. The kingdom is too glorious a reality to be marred by men as something they can create or perform. This is the reason many communities dissolve. We came into community in complete ignorance of how to do it, and that ignorance was our saving virtue. The Body of Christ is synonymous with the kingdom of God, and neither of those realities was ever intended to become institutional. Both are living organisms, built and established relationally with God and with each other. To put it another way, the glory of God is the expression of His life organically administered, through the brethren, by His Spirit, to each other. In true fellowship, the brethren are made perfect, through daily relationship, through encouraging one another and often through rebuke and confrontation:

> But encourage one another day after day, as long as it is still called "Today," so that none of you will be hardened by the deceitfulness of sin.[2]

> What we have seen and heard we proclaim to you also, so that you too may have fellowship with us; and indeed our

---

[2] Hebrews 3:13

> fellowship is with the Father, and with His Son Jesus Christ.[3]
>
> But if we walk in the Light as He Himself is in the Light, we have fellowship with one another, and the blood of Jesus His Son cleanses us from all sin.[4]

Church as community is radically and excruciatingly demanding, and yet, in this environment, there is the glorious possibility for this kind of existential fellowship with believers. As I have said, we do not have to be on the same property, although that should be preferred, but we do need to be in an intensive, frequent, honest, open-hearted and committed relationship with God's people. It will be agonizing before it is blessed, and painful before it is glorious.

In the daily life of the community, our supposed love for God is tested to the full by how much love we show for the brethren. In the wisdom and genius of God, we are saved from insisting that we can enjoy an exclusive relationship with God, while, at the same time, living separated from the brethren. Our love for God is revealed in the way we express our love to the brethren. It is *because* of that joining with the brethren and *because* God is joined with us in that kind of covenant relationship that we see the daily unfolding of His life. This unfolding will likely be slow, painful, clumsy, time-consuming and often wasteful, but the end thereof opens up the possibility for His glory to be in the church.

---

[3] 1 John 1:3
[4] 1 John 1:7

The Revelation of our Hearts

There is nothing more important than destroying romantic illusions and fantasies about what we think church as community is. The idea of joining a community of believers lends itself to either total rejection, for fear of becoming a heretical sect, or it is seen as some kind of romantic illusion of tripping off into the rustic wilds. These are terrible distortions, and if there is any romantic idealization of what community is going to confer, or mean for us, we are already in the place of unreality and deception. The enjoyment and appreciation of Christian fellowship with all of its failures and inconveniences, while we are in the process of growing up together, is a much more realistic view of church as community.

Conducting our lives on a daily basis in close proximity to others guarantees that there will be tensions, misunderstandings, individual subjectivities, struggles and differences of opinion. Our disrespect for one another, our rebellion toward authority, our innate selfishness and insidious self-justifications are all revealed. It is a painful but necessary revelation of our hearts. We have to pass through a valley of disillusionment of what we think true fellowship is, what we as God's people are, and not the least, what we ourselves are capable of. In fact, the most painful revelation we need to face is the truth of our own condition. True fellowship is the courage and the willingness to be with one another and bear with one another in all of the above conditions.

There is an ideal, but there is also a reality, and poison is injected into the fellowship when someone comes to a community on the basis of an ideal. If we seek anything more than Christian fellowship and that "more" is a projection of our own imagining and romantic hopes, then we introduce a leaven into the whole corporate lump, and by so doing, the seeds of destruction of that fellowship will have been sown. To one degree or another, we are all dreamers and idealists about what we think community ought to be, and if it does not become *that*, we become disillusioned.

In community, our vain illusions will be quickly shattered. But disillusionment is a grace from God, and the only way to be disillusioned is unhappily a painful way, but far more painful and far more disastrous is to continue in an illusion that is unreal, and which, at the judgment seat of Christ, must be revealed as false. The disillusionment is not just with others; it is recognizing things about yourself that you would not have otherwise been compelled to experience or to see. When it does reveal itself, can we then bear the pain of watching the unraveling of the illusions of another, knowing that we are not to falsely comfort them, or intervene, thus interrupting the redemptive process of God? Can we let the mortification have its full work, and bear the stink of it, while we are alongside that suffering person?

The church is the "pillar and support of truth,"[5] and if it is not that, then it is not the church in any true way. Truth has got to be unsparing and total. We cannot allow latitude for illusions and idealism, or any other kind of humanistic tendency. Church as community serves the purpose of putting those things to death. More than one community has been dissolved because the people could not survive the disillusionment. They were unprepared for it, and when it came, it took them by surprise and became the

---

[5] 1 Timothy 3:15

end for them because they had wanted to hold on to their illusions.

If we cannot endure a look of indifference, or a seeming rejection, or if we find ourselves reacting in a touchy and hypersensitive manner, how then are we going to be overcomers in the crisis time of the last days when the wrath of the powers of darkness will be ventilated against God's people in a concentrated way? If we have protective little self-centered egos underlying an outward appearance of spirituality, we will find ourselves constantly hurt, but better to recognize that now, and to submit to the sanctifying work of God in an environment of true fellowship.

Community as Organism

We cannot come into community with our own agenda; we simply come in obedience. It was the same call to Abraham: "Go forth…to the land which I will show you."[6] We come as the broken people of God, desiring to relinquish any strength which we might have in ourselves, and look to Him for the unfolding of the life together, day by day, as it pleases Him to bestow. The things that have their origin in God must have their outworking by the impartation of His life, given to those who are called together, and who respond in obedience to the direction of God.

The worst thing that anyone could do is establish community as a system in a pre-packaged way. By that, we will have contradicted the very spirit of community. Anything that is a system is antithetical to God in every point and particular. System suggests something man makes in his own wisdom and

---

[6] See Genesis 12:1

12

organizational ability, based on his own values, for the purposes of his own efficiency and success. Denominationalism is religion as system; it operates through a hierarchy of men and officers who have charge over districts and spheres of influence. We will be continually tempted to systematize our church life and bring it under human arrangement. Though it may have begun rightly, it can harden and stiffen in its forms and become an institution with a life unto itself, and thereafter, the whole issue becomes the perpetuation of the fellowship or the institution.

In antithesis to this, God has a purpose for the church that completely eclipses this mindset. He totally ignores the wisdom of the world, considering it foolish, and establishes a set of values, which in the eyes of mankind seem totally threatening, offensive, and will likely rub them raw. In the community of God's people, Christ is the Lord and center of all. It is He who mediates the life. He is King, and His Lordship is pervasive over all. His Lordship is not a body of rules that He sets down; but rather, it is something we learn of Him in the walking out of the life of faith.

The world values efficiency and utility, but in the kingdom, the values are the obtainment of godly character through whatever cost that might entail. God's main purpose is character growth, corporate life, the relationship by the Spirit, bearing one another's sufferings, and the instruction that comes to everyone because of all that. It is naïve to expect that everyone walks fully by the Spirit. A system based on efficiency will need rules and regulations to enforce it, thereby making it a legal system of telling people what to do and how. There is a tension of needing to have *some* measure of order and coherence, and yet not enforcing or requiring it, or else we would prevent the subtle tendrils of self-interest from being exposed. For example, was the failure of one of the families to pay their monthly rent actually due to poverty, or was their lifestyle and mindset of such a kind that paying rent was given little or no priority?

By the very nature of community, one's lifestyle comes under close scrutiny. The groceries we buy, the cars we drive, and the indulgences we insist we need are observed by those around us, who are committed to call us to account. It is amazing what people will spend their money on, even seeming legitimate things, but at the same time ignoring their financial responsibilities. There is a terrible tension while we patiently wait for believers to grow up to a place of maturity and responsibility, while yet resisting the temptation to try to have that measure of order by imposition.

God is concerned with optimum character development, which cannot be compelled, defined or structured. What men will do freely before God, unobserved by man, is where the real foundations of character are laid. God is interested in what is wrought in the interaction with the brethren when selfishness, vanity and pride surface in the working out of issues that come up. The "Sunday Church" mentality can easily become a mere convenience, but community is profoundly inconvenient; it is the going from "house to house daily breaking bread"[7] and working through issues, tensions, difficulties and misunderstandings. It is amazing how easily these are expressed, and how quickly they can bring to nothing a relationship that has been years in the making; all the more reason, therefore, to be in a place of daily vigilance, prayer and dependency upon God.

---

[7] See Acts 2:46

The violating of one's privacy will test us to the depths of our being. In community our privacy *will be* invaded; we will never know when someone is going to come to the door for some requirement. One of the great tensions is in discerning how much time belongs to the family and how much to the brethren. How much should we be *apart* from the community, and how much do we give ourselves to the purposes of the community? It is not stated as some written credo, but something that needs to be worked out as the days unfold. We should profoundly desire the autonomy of families with the father as the head and the integrity of the family unit, but some of the deepest forms of selfishness have been hidden under the supposed sanctity of family: "Well, I cannot come to the meeting because of the children." How much has that been used as an excuse for people who really do not want to assemble together, and are employing the sanctity of family, as well as other values, as a cover behind which to hide?

Everything about true fellowship needs to be mediated from heaven by the Holy Spirit; it was so at the inauguration of the church and needs to be so now.

> And behold, I am sending forth the promise
> of My Father upon you; but you are to stay
> in the city [Jerusalem] until you are clothed
> with power from on high.[8]

The Spirit was never given for us to do great acts that would distinguish us *as individuals*. He was sent to be the power and enablement for the corporate life together out of which those acts would then flow. In coming into community, it takes only a few weeks before you realize that you are not the nice guy you thought you were. True fellowship is based on His

---

[8] Luke 24:49

15

life, His resurrection life, which is His power, and yet there are so few who live in that realm, or who actually desire to.   In fact, our present Christianity and conventional lifestyles, however well-meaning and disciplined, rarely require us to cross over into that realm, but as soon as we come into a testing relationship with each other, we will find that we will need to know the reality of His life.

Let God make community in His own image, not what *we* think it should be. It may well be that His image for each of us is unique to ourselves, and the thing that most deters true fellowship from fulfillment is our insistence that the fellowship should conform to *our* image. May God give us such a heart for truth and authenticity, and to be made *corporately* into His image, for it is this that glorifies Him.

Chapter 2

The Body of Christ

The Body of Christ is an eternal masterpiece, and I do not think we have sufficiently appreciated God's intention for it, nor have we shown much of the respect and esteem that the Body rightly deserves. We seem to look at each other rather inadequately, and this must have something to do, in part, with our inability to discern the Body, where there is a kind of matter-of-fact, half-hearted attitude of indifference toward one another. We do not esteem Christ in His people, nor do we esteem the variety of God's people with all of their inherent differences. We are selective, and more responsive and partial to those who are like ourselves, and consequently we miss seeing the fullness of Christ in His Body.

Discerning the Body requires a revelation, and here again we stand in danger of taking something very holy and making it a commonplace. We can employ the phrase "the Body of Christ" but does that mean we have a true understanding of it? For me, the revelation of the Body came out of the struggle with my own wife in trying to reconcile Jew and Gentile, male and female. There are multitudes of contradictions represented right there, but the glory of God is most revealed in the taking of two opposite persons and making of them one new man, one new entity.[1] It is in the antagonism, in the friction, and in the issues of reconciliation that one begins to glimpse something of the genius of what the Body is as a living organism in all of its diversity and differences.

The Body of Christ is not to be mistaken for the institutional use of that word. Even in charismatic and evangelical churches there is often an institutional mentality and mindset. On account of the casual manner of our language and the lack of discerning the Body, we talk about unity in the Body of Christ as meaning some kind of ecumenical coming together of Catholics and Protestants, or different denominations coming to some common organizational agreement. I do not have a word sufficient to describe that distortion. It is certainly a caricature of the divine intention, and it stems from the error of mindlessly using the phrase: the Body of Christ. The Body is a living organism in the intention of God, sacred and holy, and only as an organism does it have a life that flows down from the Head to which it is joined. Such an authentic Body, unobtrusive and unrecognized by the world, will always be an object of collision and opposition to the institutional model.

> And He gave some as apostles, and some as
> prophets, and some as evangelists, and some
> as pastors and teachers, for the equipping of

---

[1] See Ephesians 2:15

the saints for the work of service, for the building up of the Body of Christ.[2]

It is little wonder that the institutional church, by whatever name it is called, does not respond hospitably to God-sent apostles and prophets. Institutions demand that you go through a credentializing process by attending schools and seminaries. From then on, you get labeled evangelist, pastor or teacher, and get fitted into the institutional framework, but that does not mean God recognizes or authenticates your service for Him. The true Body of Christ will recognize and receive what is organically fitted for itself, and will reject the thing that is organically alien. The opposite is equally true: the institutional model cannot accommodate and receive the organic entity; they are diametrically opposed to each other.

The purposes of God that pertain to His coming, His kingdom and His eternal glory will only be performed through His Body, and yet this organic entity, by its very nature, requires such a painful process to obtain the fullness that God is wanting.

> Until we all attain to the unity of the faith, and of the knowledge of the Son of God, to a mature man, to the measure of the stature which belongs to the fullness of Christ. As a result, we are no longer to be children, tossed here and there by waves and carried about by every wind of doctrine, by the trickery of men, by craftiness in deceitful scheming; but speaking the truth in love, we are to grow up in all aspects into Him who is the head, even Christ, from whom the whole body, being fitted and held together by what every joint supplies, according to

---

[2] Ephesians 4:11-12

the proper working of each individual part,
causes the growth of the body for the
building up of itself in love.[3]

Speaking the truth in love is an absolute necessity, but it can be avoided in any fellowship that is not constituted as an organic expression of the Body. You can go to meetings in that kind of fellowship for a lifetime, and never once be required to speak the truth in love; but once you come into the Body, then it becomes virtually a daily necessity. The process of growth comes by what we ourselves provide to each other. The supply comes from the Head to impart life to the Body, but we can block that life by being minimal with each other. It shows in the way we give so little to each other of our time, our attention, our gifts and our finances. The Lord is looking for a generosity of spirit that fills the house with the fragrance of Himself. We should be giving a lavish overflow to the Body because we esteem the Head to which it is joined as being one divine organism. I am always asking people, "To what expression of the Body are you joined?" This is different from asking, "What church do you attend?" The church you attend may be the place of your ministry and service as a mission field. If we are not joined to an expression of the Body, we are losing the flow of life from the Head.

In the Body of Christ, there is no room for passivity on the part of each member:

When you assemble, each one has a psalm,
has a teaching, has a revelation, has a
tongue, has an interpretation. Let all things
be done for edification.[4]

---

[3] Ephesians 4:13-16
[4] 1 Corinthians 14:26b

The life of the Body is expressed to the Body whenever it assembles together for the edification and growth of that Body. Not too many churches encourage that kind of open format, preferring a trained and salaried minister to arrange and conduct the service. We may even find that we are more than willing to pay the cost of his salary in order that we might be absolved from the spiritual responsibility of having to share a psalm, a teaching, a revelation, a tongue or an interpretation! Consequently, the Body is emaciated. Being inadequately fed, it cannot grow, and we are therefore limp, disjointed and anemic. If this life-giving provision is not expressed, we will be left severely weakened, with many of us sick and dying. In the Body, there can be no excuse to justify our inactivity and passivity. When we come together, we should have prepared ourselves already in the place of prayer, fully expecting that God is going to quicken and bring something through us for the growth and edification of the Body.

When Paul came back a year or two later to those places where he had established churches, he had only to appoint elders. It was not some capricious choice; there was an instant recognition of the ones whom God had already promoted. He saw the maturity that was already evidenced in certain men. He saw those who had risen to assume responsibility so as to oversee and shepherd others, and he laid hands on them and prayed for them in the presence of the Body, and, by that act, they were recognized and established as elders. The expression of the Body in those localities grew and matured during Paul's absence because each one had a psalm, a teaching, revelation, a tongue and an interpretation.

The Unity of the Body

True unity is not cheap, nor is it something we can enforce or establish politically. Once it is obtained, we need to jealously guard and maintain it. Dwelling together indicates something more than a transient moment; it is a consistent mode of being that requires remarkable investment to obtain. The precious oil of anointing that comes down from above is not the statement of our individual virtuosity or singular callings, but what we enjoy because of our relationship together. But if we have an individualistic mindset, especially about our own calling, gift and ministry, we will hold the view that anointing is relative to *our* gift. The anointing of God, which is the life of God and the power of God, is the issue of our relatedness to the Body that dwells together in unity. It was true at the first, and it will be true again at the last.

> And with great power the apostles were giving testimony to the resurrection of the Lord Jesus, and abundant grace was upon them all.[5]

The abundant grace upon them was the presence of God's Spirit. They were a people tempered *together*, not merely alongside of each other, and there was a oneness that was more than mere human congeniality. True unity comes from the ability to suffer each other in our failures, infirmities, weaknesses and humiliations. It is nurtured in an environment that is loving, that allows for failure and error, but does not condemn. It sees the weakness and demerit of the brother, and speaks to Christ about him in prayer.

---

[5] Acts 4:33

If the early apostles were not dwelling together in unity, they would not have had enough power to inflate a balloon, let alone bring the gospel to the same Jewish community that had so recently crucified the Messiah. This quality of unity will not come to us except we break through the stifling structures that have been ours historically, which are predicated upon conventional Sunday services and mid-week Bible studies. To come to this unity is not some ecumenical design that is going to be established on a platform by the religious skill of men, but by those who are willing to pay the price for it in the necessary redemptive suffering that alone obtains it. This is not an option or an alternative, but the definitive desire of God from the first, for all generations, and especially the last.

Chapter 3

The Suffering before the Glory

Community living is the place where you abandon all hope for the continuation of your carnal, fleshly tendencies. It is precisely for this reason that such a living arrangement is shunned, despised and spoken against. Institutional church, as organized religion in whatever forms it takes, delights in hearing of the failures of communities. They are thereby confirmed in their own structured life, and they will say, "Well, community can never work. Yes, at the beginning of the church age, and because of persecution, it was necessary that they shared their possessions and had all things in common, but that can never work today." In essence, they do not *want* it to work, and they are only too delighted to hear the reports when such attempts fail and collapse.

In community, we have to bear the painful embarrassment of having our weaknesses exposed for all to see. You may be a great preacher at those public speaking engagements, and under the anointing of

God, but how are you at home with the wife and children? In community, all our inadequacies are revealed, but our willingness to bear those painful sufferings allows for a glimpse and a revealing of the glory that always follows.

Jesus endured all of His suffering for the joy that was set before Him. He saw and anticipated what would be the consequences of His obedient sufferings for all eternity; and that is what we need to see too. The wisdom that can rejoice in suffering is a virtual contradiction in terms; it is contrary to our every reasoning and to everything we think natural and normal to man. It is the wisdom of God, but it needs to be demonstrated by a fellowship whose inner life is itself the proclamation of God's wisdom. It is a wisdom that is worked in us through trial and testing, and in the struggles of relationships. Every impulse is to run off to the first charismatic or evangelical fellowship you can find, just to be relieved from the tension of all of the demands. However, it is precisely in those tensions that God can most readily form His character.

The Dealings of God

In community, we have seen the unraveling of exceptional believers, those who have given up their businesses and homes, and come to our rugged northern Minnesotan environment with its extremely long and cold winters. Back home, they were considered head and shoulders above their fellows, and yet, this did not save them from the dealings of God when they came into the matrix of community life. We watched them acting in ways that they would have never thought themselves capable of, and as they came into the miserable, wretched agony of "death," we who were with them were required to bear the reproach of it until that death had done its full work.

I remember a brother going through what I am describing. As we were coming back from a meeting, we passed his house, and my wife said, "Why don't you go in and comfort him. After all, you are in the place of responsibility." I said, "Yeah, that's a good idea," and started to turn, but that was as far as I got. The Lord was not going to allow me to interfere with the process of death being worked in him by bringing a premature and false comfort, when comfort was not what was required. This man had to taste that death to the full, and he did, and there was a glorious deliverance later that came because we did not interfere. In other words, we need discretion, discernment and to be led of the Spirit, which is also the issue of the maturity of the elders and whether the Lord has had His full work in them. No one can come to this maturity by himself, but in the daily interaction with the brethren, and in their own receiving of correction and counsel, even from the least of the flock, the leaders come increasingly into being a Spirit-led people.

Speaking the Truth

Truth is costly in its demands, and that is why only the lovers of truth are saved from deception. We have got to love truth in order to be true. It is not just the truth of our doctrines; we ourselves need to be true through and through, in our attitudes, our speech, our eyes and our thoughts. With all of the compromise in the world and the church, we need a daily vigilance. We cannot see our blind spots, the sins that so easily beset us. We need the word of truth from the brethren to reveal them to us. Will we be humble enough to receive the word when it comes from them, or will we be resentful? True humility is submitting, not only to the most mature believers in the fellowship, but also to the weakest, the immature and the youngest. Will we recognize and receive from their mouths the word of God for *us*?

We need a jealousy for truth, and courage to speak the whole truth, no matter what the consequence. We must have a love of the truth beyond our desire for success as ministers, beyond our desire for the success of our denominations and fellowships. Our love for God is no greater than our love for truth. Do not measure your love for God by your rapturous euphoria in an imagined relationship with the Lord that has been stimulated by choruses and worship. That would be a deception. What is our naked love of truth in the cold, gray dawn of the new day when things are not as convenient as we would like? That would be a truer measure of our love for God. Truth is costly, and if we will not die for it, we do not really love it. Truth is not an abstract thing separate from God, nor is it truth *about* God. Love of the truth has got to be cultivated and nurtured; therefore, we need to live in an environment that cherishes truth, that will not tolerate the lie, or allow the cutting of corners. We are not sufficient for that in ourselves, and therefore we need the brethren on a daily basis.

I remember speaking to a fellowship where three of the leading women had left their husbands and were living in adulterous relationships. They had disgraced the entire fellowship, thc name of God, and the reputation of that fellowship in its community. At what point did the first leaven of the deceitfulness of sin come to these women? Sin disguises itself; that is what makes it deceitful. It conceals its own character as sin, operating instead as justifiable desire. How was it that those who were related to these women did not discern it? Why were they not found out earlier when their first disposition for flirting was seen and recognized? There should have been someone to say, "Sister, I detect something in your eyes, your voice and in your teasing and flattering way with men that is not appropriate for a believer. I do not feel that you should be expressing yourself in this unseemly way." A little leaven will eventually corrupt the entire lump. To love truth is to love the truth of the cross; it is to welcome with joy the humiliation of suffering the indignity of being corrected and reproved, and having questions raised about yourself that you have an obligation to consider. Are we willing to hear that painful kind of word from one another? Are we willing to speak it? The one is just as much the cross as the other.

In Galatians 2:11, we read that Paul did not hold back from confronting Peter concerning his inconsistencies. Apparently Peter was one kind of believer when he was with the Gentiles and quite another when the Jews came. There was duplicity and deceitfulness in his conduct that was already compromising the gospel. Paul confronted him to his face, before the brethren, for the sake of the purity of the gospel. Paul showed Peter a deception that was already beguiling Barnabas, as well as others who were being brought into the same deception. How would we like to be in the days of the early church again, where, if we begin to offer something that is not completely true, and yet make it to appear as true, we would be struck dead and carried out feet first? How would we like *that* kind of judgment to come again to the church? In the environment of truth and speaking the truth in love, the church *then* was a powerful witness, and it says that "great fear came over the whole church, and over all who heard of these things."[1]

It was Peter who had discerned in Ananias and Sapphira that they were only giving in part, yet the same Peter was confronted by Paul later on in his walk with God. The one who was mightily used of God to discern the lie and compromise of another had begun to practice his own deception, and needed himself to be corrected. The person who thinks he is immune from deception is the greatest candidate *for* deception.

This may well be why so many of our leading tele-evangelists and charismatic personalities fall into shameful sin. Where were those who could have confronted them earlier on, when the first signs of something wrong were beginning to show themselves? Were these ministers living in fellowship in the apostolic context that I am describing, or were they in a more institutional arrangement surrounded by paid staff who habitually affirmed them? Would they have been willing to live in a closely-knit body of believers, where the youngest and weakest member could have been the instrument of bringing correction to them?

I often exhort fellowships to watch for a change in their pastor's voice and inflection. If the reality of his speaking becomes professional, studied and affected, he needs to be told, because he himself is not likely to be aware of it. You can slip from being the authentic man, speaking unaffectedly out of the truth of your life and knowledge, to becoming increasingly a performer of a religious kind. But the man himself will not likely be aware unless he is told. How will he be told? You just have to say: "I have to tell you that when I hear you now, I have a strange discomfort in my spirit. I cannot quite identify it, but there is something coming

---

[1] Acts 5:11

29

into your speaking, an inflection in your voice that for the lack of a better word sounds professional. Your words and your voice are losing the sound of reality. You were so natural and unaffected before, but now you sound metallic. Forgive me if I am missing this, but I feel like I need to express that." This is speaking the truth in love. Wherever something of that critical a kind is identified and addressed in its inception by someone who has the courage, love and sensitivity to the Spirit, then right there is true fellowship. We need those who can speak such things, and we need to receive them when they are spoken *to us*. If we only speak the truth in a critical way, it will not have any redemptive value.

One of the ways of distinguishing a true love of God from the false human thing is by ascertaining what end it serves. If there is a ploy, a device or a maneuver to win something for oneself in a self-serving way, then it is not true love. It can take place in marriage where both partners are happily benefiting from the self-serving and mutual compatibility and enjoyment that they have together. But when the romantic illusion is tested, the supposed love *will* turn to hatred because the true reality does not conform to the expectation. The love that was never a true love cannot stand the failure; it was a love of love, rather than the love of the person, and in the sense of betrayal and disappointment, the false love must necessarily turn to hatred.

If we have been operating like that in our marriages, what shall we expect in our fellowships? There is a remarkable corollary between the allowance of illusion in the realm of our private or married life, and what we bring into our fellowships. We need to have in both an uttermost authenticity and reality. Do we have enough real love for one another that we will pierce the bubble of phony and deceitful things, and speak the truth in love? This is the kind of love that God wants to be expressed in His Body because it is in perfect conjunction with truth. The love of truth and the love of God are one and the same. It takes a supreme jealousy for authenticity in the fellowship, without which there will be no glory unto God. On the other hand, can we be loving enough to *withhold* speaking, and remain silent when we may seem justified in bringing a word of correction? Whether it is to bring correction or to withhold, true love requires a discernment and discipline appropriate for each occasion.

Face to Face

We need to be in an authentic expression of the Body of Christ where we can submit our life, character and conduct to the authority and members in that Body. It may not be with a regular church fellowship *per se*. You may find it in a Bible study group, or in an informal gathering of people who meet frequently, and who are earnestly seeking to go on with God. You will receive what you need for your growth and maturity from those with whom you are in daily or frequent face to face relationship. If we will not meet with each other face to face, it is a sign that we have little regard to seek the face of God.

Our desire to see the glory of God in the church does not mean that it is going to take place automatically. Many of us are content to *talk* about the glory of God without any realistic expectation of seeing that glory. In many of our secret hearts, where we hardly know our own motives, there are deep-rooted desires for our own ministerial or religious success and the perpetuation of our ministries. Such would have very little desire to seek to come into that matrix of life whereby the glory of God can be expressed. Very few of God's people want to face the issues of truth in any intensive way. That is why we have fellowships that prefer to turn up the amplifiers, establish and promote worship leaders, and employ music to bring the sense of a spiritual euphoria and the impression of an alive church, but without the foundational and unmistakable reality of true fellowship. A good definition of much of present Christendom is that it wants the *sense* of the power and gifts of God, but without the cross of God. Truth is powerful; it makes a requirement; it is challenging and brings conviction. Truth calls us *to the cross*.

More often than not, there is an unspoken agreement between pastors and their flock: "You present a biblical message; we will pay the bill and have a Sunday service that will leave our lives free from any kind of demand that would *really* touch our true vested interests and values." In other words, we do not want a message that is going to reveal where our hearts really are.

Our school education systems are content with the mere verbalization of material; they want to know how able you are to repeat it back for them without the actualizing of that knowledge. When we bring this mentality into the faith, we assume that the verbal recitation or agreement with a doctrine means that we have the corresponding reality. But this would be a credal faith rather than an existential one. We have not been made sufficiently aware that there is a needful existential and authentic appropriation of the faith in order for there to be true faith.

We need also to discern by the Spirit who it is that the *Lord* is sending to us to form the environment of true fellowship. You do not have to be mature; you do not have to be a great disciple; you do not have to come with any money; you simply come. The only question is, "Has God sent you?" The person needs to know that, and the fellowship needs to know, because there will be trials and demanding conditions, but if you know that you are called, then you can bear any trial that comes. We should be so complete in our trust of God's sovereignty that no matter what happens, we will receive it with complete peace, equanimity and joy. Are we at that place now? Would we ever come to that place except by the only way it can be obtained, namely, through the sacrifice and suffering *in* the Body of Christ, *in* an intensity of life together, *in* the give-and-take, and *in* the grit of tensions and dealings?

Chapter 4

The Mystery of Suffering

Coming into true fellowship is conditional upon our appropriation of the meaning of the suffering unto death of Jesus at the cross of Calvary. There is no other event in time that more reveals God as He in fact is, and there is a mystery here that we need to be apprehended by, and that needs to register deeply in our consciousness. If we are too glib in expressing our knowledge of the cross, or if we seem to have neatly nailed it down and can quote statements about it, then we have in all probability missed the meaning and mystery of the anguish, the blood, the suffering, and the glory of all that inheres in the cross.

Many of us are guilty of making God into *our* image. A projection takes place in our minds when we hear the name of Jesus mentioned, and probably every one of us has a variation on who we think Jesus is. If our Jesus is any other than He who was crucified and rose again, then it is a self-serving Jesus, not the sacrificial Lamb of God. We need to know Him exactly as He is, and He is nowhere presented more accurately as the reflection and image of God than in His suffering unto death.

The root of all of our ills, strife, divisions, fears, jealousies, ambitions and everything that leads to the rupture and fragmentation of marriages and fellowships is due to our failure to radically apprehend God as He is. Though our voices may become rapturous and our emotions titillated in mentioning the name of Jesus, to what degree are we celebrating the crucified and risen Christ? And to what degree are we just singing a song to a blurred image of our own making that serves our own vested self-interests and well-being? False images *will* lead to things false in our own lives, and they can only be corrected by knowing God as He is, where He has presented Himself unsparingly and accurately in the suffering and death of His Son.

In fact, nothing is more grossly neglected in modern Christendom than the cross of Christ Jesus, and we have suffered enormously for the avoidance of this subject. The cross itself is ruthless and absolute. It is an unswerving standard, a plumb line from God by which everything must be conformed and measured. If it is absent, or has been neglected, or some other substitute has been put in its place, though we allude to it as the cross, if it be not *the* cross of the crucified Christ, then *everything* in our spiritual life will be at variance.

The word "suffering" is as much neglected and misunderstood as the word "cross" and for exactly the same reasons. The suffering of the cross is the suffering of dying; the way of the cross is the way of abandonment. Death is a synonym for suffering, and every suffering is a humiliation. Living in a civilization that has little or no tolerance for pain, the thought of suffering is considered a morbid subject, and anyone who introduces it must therefore necessarily be of a masochistic bent. "To choose suffering is a disease; but to choose God's will, even though it means suffering, is to suffer as Jesus did, according to the will of God."[1] Suffering for Christ's sake is another kind of suffering; it is a redemptive suffering, and there is a peculiar and particular grace that accompanies it that is a joy unspeakable and full of glory.

The Nature of Suffering

There is an inherent unwillingness in man to make peace with the cross, and an unwillingness to recognize that the way of faith *is* the way of suffering. It is the prospect of suffering that intimidates us more than the suffering itself. It is not so much the actual death that scares God's people, as the *fear* of death. How many of our rationales and justifications for keeping ourselves from the intensity of relationship with the people of God really stem from our fear of being found out, afraid to fail before the eyes of others, afraid to suffer the humiliation? And therefore we gird ourselves about with every kind of justification to safely distance ourselves from any possibility of that prospect.

It is for this reason that we have not exhibited what necessarily must follow entry into the sufferings of Christ, namely, resurrection life. God waits for an anguished cry from us, rather than easy and glib words about a phenomenon that is at the heart of the faith. The sooner we acknowledge that we do not have the resurrection reality, and be thrust into the despair that

---

[1] Oswald Chambers—*Living Water*

we rightly deserve, the sooner we shall enter the reality of that life. Ironically, there is nothing that more militates *against* that reality than our religious activity and our inadequate knowledge of God. God waits for the recognition that we are imprisoned and bound up, and that we have not attained to the actuality of which we speak.

The cross is not the cross until we have experienced it as utter abandonment. How many of us have misinterpreted the circumstances that God is currently bringing into our lives, and have attributed them to the enemy, or to the consequences of our own doings? How many of us are seeking valiantly to do everything to avoid our coming into this sense of utter forlornness and abandonment, where we are bereft even of what we thought we knew and understood the faith to be?

When Jesus was impaled upon the cross, a great darkness came over the earth.[2] How many of us would be willing for great darkness and great nothingness to come upon *us*? Even to the point where the doctrines of which we are so assured should also be brought to nothing? The darkness that covered Jesus upon the cross must come upon us also as a negation of *all* things, even those things which we think we have understood about the cross itself.

Are we willing to come to that utter destitution of soul where even though what we say might be true, it has yet, for too many of us, not been *made* true, and *will* not and *cannot*, until we allow this darkness to come over us? God is waiting for us to divest ourselves of mere biblical phrases, and to be willing to suffer a "dark night of the soul" in order to come into a true knowledge of Him and His way.

---

[2] See Matthew 27:45-46

When a Gentile centurion saw Jesus on the cross, though he had seen numbers of men squirming, groaning and cursing while being crucified, there was something about the manner of Jesus' dying that evoked this statement from his mouth: "Truly, this was the Son of God!"[3] In seeing what was exhibited in Jesus' ultimate suffering unto death, a Gentile, who likely had no biblical background, is drawn to recognize the true identity of the crucified Christ. Though Jesus had performed many miracles, it took this decisive testimony of Himself to bring what may well have constituted salvation for a man who would have otherwise eternally perished as a sinner.

"But we do see Him...namely; Jesus, because of the suffering of death crowned with glory and honor..."[4] To see Jesus in the condition of His suffering is to see the most accurate depiction of God as He is. To see Jesus is to see the glory of God, and to see the glory of God is to see Jesus. The standard of God by which He measures everything is found in the cross of Christ Jesus, in the actual experience of our lives as those who have come to Him, willing to abandon everything. We need to rend every veil that keeps us from coming into that inner sanctuary of true seeing. When we see Him as He in fact is, there is nothing left to do but to repent from our self-centered existence and from lives that bear little correspondence with His sacrificial one. Only *then* can true faith take place.

We hardly ever hear any allusion to the cross beyond atonement, but there is another dimension of the cross that enters the realm of glory for those who have received the cross as death. Why is there a

---

[3] Matthew 27:54
[4] See Hebrews 2:9

38

painful disparity between our verbal professions and the actual condition of our lives? The woeful and pathetic condition of the lives of many of God's people and their enormous fascination for the world testify to the fact that we have tragically avoided the cross of Jesus.

Do our hearts wince when we touch any aspect of the spirit and wisdom of this world? Is its wisdom as abominable to us as it is to God, not only its ugliest vices, but also those things applauded as virtuous and good that are equally of the world? "That which is highly esteemed of men is detestable in the sight of God."[5] Do we treat the world as if it is under the judgment of God? Do we see *all* of its aspects, including its culture and the things that are imposing, elegant and honorific, as also having their origin in hell, and being ruled over by the prince of darkness? Is our distaste for the world such that we cannot wait to get out of it?

Paul could say that he boasted *only* in the cross of Jesus Christ, through which the world had been crucified to him, and he to the world.[6] Nothing less than the cross can separate us from a world that is powerfully seductive and at enmity with God. Only the cross can effectually crucify the world from us and us from it.

Denying Self

Jesus said, "If anyone wishes to come after Me, he must deny himself, and take up his cross and follow Me."[7] Dietrich Bonhoeffer likened the call of God to a

---

[5] Luke 16:15b
[6] See Galatians 6:14
[7] Matthew 16:24b

man as being an invitation to come and die. For those who hear that call, the cross is the power of God as expressed in resurrection life. Having come, we invite upon ourselves the daily dying, the daily reiteration of this mystery in ways that are uniquely appropriate to our lives, our call and our walk. If the cross is not operative daily, if we are not willing to suffer its deaths, for example, when our flesh rises up and we find a way to skirt around an issue, then we make ourselves, to that degree, candidates for sin and deception.

The issue of being saved from deception is the issue of the cross. It is the issue of our willingness to be ruthless with regard to ourselves, bearing the suffering of it when God makes the issue clear. If we are escapists, running from confrontation, rationalizing and justifying our conduct and finding a way to explain it that gratifies us and saves us from the acknowledgement of sin as sin, then we are to that degree candidates for deception. The love of the truth is the only thing that saves us from deception, and the most acute expression of that truth is Christ and Him crucified.

The individual who moves away from the cross, who allows the cross to be only a ceremonial and architectural decoration, who is not willing for the suffering of the cross, or living a cruciform life, makes himself a candidate for deception. The deception will likely come from very God Himself, who will give lying delusions to those who have rejected the love of the truth. Mere tolerance for the truth and respect for the truth are not enough.

God is the God of truth, and anything that is feigned, phony and an affectation is a lie. It is far better that we suffer the knowing of our true condition than that we should live deceptive lives before God and man. We can play it safe and live our lives secretly and privately, and be a little island in the midst of the crowd, or we can open ourselves to the redemptive work of God that comes in the fellowship of His people. We can love truth, seek truth, pursue truth and suffer for the truth, or we can play it safe and live by the conventional and moral standards of the world.

Through suffering, we can come increasingly into the abounding joy and glory of the Lord, none of which can ever be the experience of those who void this process. It is painful to deny ourselves anything. If anyone were to walk into our church services, our heads automatically turn to look; we have *got* to *see*; we have got to hear; the silence has got to be filled; our mind has got to be engaged; our fingers have got to be occupied. The denial of self in any form is a painful suffering, and many of us are still unable and unwilling to face the issue of its pain. The avoidance of pain is a costly avoidance, and the reality of the cross is an invitation to share in His sufferings. In the avoidance of the cross of Christ Jesus, our contemporary church life is really nothing more than a culture, a sanctifying cover-up for the *status quo*, a vacuous praise club, attributing gain as godliness and a comfortable religiosity that leaves our real interests unchallenged and undisturbed.

Paul wrote: "For I determined to know nothing among you except Jesus Christ, and Him crucified."[8] It is amazing how our intellect likes to *know* many things just for the sake of knowing. To deny your mind the pleasure of contemplating what it chooses is itself an exercise in suffering. Any act of self-denial is an exercise in suffering, and we need to encourage one

---

[8] 1Corinthians 2:2

another to welcome the inherent centrality of suffering as being part and parcel of normative Christian living.

The Consequences of the Cross

What is a pastor going to do with a carnal congregation that brings into the meetings its dead weight and grayness? If he wants to have a "successful" service, he will find himself yielding more and more to a spirit of manipulation in order to produce some semblance of life. (Manipulation is the antithesis of faith, and it is a scandal and a shame that many of our services, particularly in the Charismatic and Pentecostal realm, look like High School football rallies and attempts to pump up flesh in the guise of spirituality. How many of us even see this as an avoidance of the cross, or are we quite comfortable with that environment? >

Waiting on God in silence would reveal the truth of our spiritual bankruptcy, but instead we drown it out with our amplifiers and ceaseless activity. There is a reason we are uncomfortable with silence. There is often a tacit and unspoken agreement between ministers and congregations by which the show goes on for the preservation of a safe *status quo*, while carnality and sin abound unchecked and unaddressed in the lives of both the congregants and the ministers. In the name of being defenders of the faith, we find fearful men actually opposing it, even the shepherds who consider themselves the most vigilant guardians of the faith and their flocks, not having been existentially apprehended by the dynamic of the cross.

The spontaneity of the leading of the Holy Spirit hardens into a fixed liturgy of choruses, followed by dramatic pauses, and, depending where you are, followed by pontifical prophecies that are of the most general kind that you would hardly think God would even bother to speak. They are accepted for the nothing things that they are, because we go right on with business as usual without being in any way affected. The whole thing becomes mere performance, and our nonchalance is itself the proof of what our real attitude is.

Jesus brought His death upon Himself by His own character, life and message. What then shall be brought upon us if we desire to be formed into His character, move in His life and proclaim His message? The disposition that clamors for prosperity, for blessings and the rapture-as-escape theory is not the spirit that is going to appreciate a message on suffering and the cross.

The cross should be the central and pivotal event of all our life and faith. In the daytime of our comfortable, religious understanding, all must go dark for us and become as night. We have become too used to the cross, and have made of it only a theory and formula for salvation. We have come to altar call after altar call, invitation after invitation, laying our lives down before Christ again and again, and yet we are still very much alive. The veil of selfishness, self-interest, vanity and pride is still not rent. The rocks of our hearts are still not split. Where has been the revelatory event of the cross of Christ *for us*?

The crucifixion of Jesus, the ending in shameful nakedness of a life that began in nakedness, is the complete negation of every kind of conventional wisdom and religious notion that mankind could conjure. By the total negation of *all* of our life, and in the yielding up of our spirits, we enter into His glory and resurrection life, which life can only be manifested through those who have been joined with Him in death and burial, who have been raised with Him into that newness of life. God will only bury that which is dead, and we will know that we have entered into the death when we see the evidence of the glory of the resurrection life.

My observation is that the overwhelming majority of God's people put confidence in their flesh and their own natural ability and aptitude to live the Christian life. We may make an impressive show of it, but it is not *newness* of life, which is an utterly supernatural reality that brings the believer thereby into a new dimension of existence, reality and life. We are *in* that life or we are *not*; God has made it absolute. Merely to employ the word "resurrection" and allude to it, quote it and preach it, does not mean that we *have* it. What is the consistent evidence of it in our lives?

> For you have died and your life is hidden with Christ in God. When Christ, who is our life, is revealed, then you also will be revealed with Him in glory.[9]

Are we willing to have our lives predicated on that basis, and are we willing to cease our efforts to get by on the strength of our own natural ability? Our life is dead *except* His life be revealed, which means we will be left humiliated *often.* When we want to shine, or to be clever, impressive and entertaining, God will not be there to accommodate us. His glory is the glory of His life, but only when He reveals it. When *His* life will be expressed by speaking, then we speak. Trusting for His life, moment by moment, is the faith for which the saints once contended and lived by.

---

[9] Colossians 3:3-4

44

Chapter 5

The Mystery of the Church

There are statements expressed in Paul's letter to the church in Ephesus that seem to create a misty aura of high-sounding concepts, without the hope of any practical or obtainable fulfillment. However, if we are to be an apostolic presence in the earth, which is to say, a true expression and fulfillment of the purposes of God, then the grand essence of what Paul is saying needs to come into our understanding. If we do not sense the ultimacy of God's eternal purposes, as expressed in this letter, we will likely be rendered inert in time; we *will* fall short of the glory of God.

In chapter 3, Paul writes about the mystery of the church. God is jealous over His mysteries, and He is not going to allow them to be mishandled, trifled with or rudely examined by those who do not have a right disposition of heart for them. There needs to be a sense of reverence and appreciation for divine mystery, and a desire that they be unveiled and revealed. The revealing of the mysteries of God is calculated to bring the church into its full apostolic constituency, and it is only as an apostolic church that divine mystery can be administered and effectually fulfilled. Mysteries are reserved for holy apostles and prophets; they must come to us through them; then the teachers can follow in order to sift and refine and show the application.

> That by revelation there was made known to me the mystery, as I wrote before in brief. By referring to this, when you read you can understand my insight into the mystery of Christ, which in other generations was not made known to the sons of men, as it has now been revealed to His holy apostles and prophets in the Spirit; to be specific, that the Gentiles are fellow heirs and fellow members of the Body, and fellow partakers of the promise in Christ Jesus through the gospel, of which I was made a minister, according to the gift of God's grace which was given to me according to the working of His power. To me, the very least of all saints...[1]

Paul actually saw himself as the least of all saints throughout his entire apostolic career, and because he saw himself as the least, he was therefore given the most; he was given the stewardship of the mysteries of God. God will not give mysteries to self-assertive and ambitious people who would use them for the advancement of their own careers and the recognition of men. The more a believer understands the ways of God, and is brought through ever-deepening humility into the reality of His mysteries and call, the more he is aware of his own nothingness.

---

[1] Ephesians 3:3-8a

One Body

The Body mentioned in verse 6 is the already existing Body of Jewish believers who never left the faith, who recognized and received the Messiah, and who received the Holy Spirit that was promised them. The mystery is that Gentiles can *now* be fellow heirs *with* them, and fellow partakers *with* them in Messiah Jesus through the gospel. The biblical faith of the God of Israel, which is the inheritance of the Jews, has now been made available to Gentiles. To be apprehended by an understanding of this mystery is calculated to defuse any proud and superior attitude in Gentiles, who might now consider the faith as being *their* Christianity. Gentiles have been allowed into something that has its roots in the God of Israel and goes back to the very inception of His redemptive history.

> Remember that you were at that time separate from Christ, excluded from the commonwealth of Israel, and strangers to the covenants of promise, having no hope and without God in the world.
>
> But now in Christ Jesus you who formerly were far off have been brought near by the blood of Christ. For He Himself is our peace, who made both groups into one and broke down the barrier of the dividing wall, by abolishing in His flesh the enmity, which is the Law of commandments contained in ordinances, so that in Himself He might make the two into one new man, thus establishing peace, and might reconcile

them both in one body to God through the
cross, by it having put to death the enmity.[2]

Gentiles, who were once without God and without
hope in the world, have been brought, by the blood of
the Messiah Jesus, into something they never had
access to before, namely, the commonwealth that
exclusively belonged to Israel. Up to that time, Jews
considered it unclean to enter a Gentile home, let alone
embrace them into the same faith. Paul reiterates this
same mystery in his letter to the Colossians:

> Of this church I was made a minister
> according to the stewardship from God
> bestowed on me for your benefit, so that I
> might fully carry out the preaching of the
> word of God, that is, the mystery which has
> been hidden from the past ages and
> generations; but has now been manifested to
> His saints, to whom God willed to make
> known what is the riches of the glory of this
> mystery among the Gentiles, which is Christ
> in you, the hope of glory.[3]

There is no contradiction between these two texts.
Gentiles are brought into the commonwealth of Israel,
into their hopes and promises, into Christ Himself.
That is how we were brought in, which is also the
same basis for Jews being brought in. It is the same
mystery expressed in yet another way. In the past,
believing Jews were in that faith and life, and now
Gentiles are brought also into that same reality. This is
not a cultural call to some judaistic thing, but to the life
of God in Messiah, in which Jewish believers and
Gentiles are joined, and made into "one new man."[4]

---

[2] Ephesians 2:12-16
[3] Colossians 1:25-27
[4] See Ephesians 2:15

In other words, God has brought Gentiles into the Hebraic root, into the life and sap of God, through the blood of the Messiah Jesus. With few exceptions, Gentiles were previously outside and excluded from the faith. But together with the believing remnant of Jews of every generation, God is making of us one new man and brings us into what we call the church.[5] By so doing, the wisdom of God is demonstrated to the powers of the air by taking Jews and Gentiles, two previously unrelated and separate groups, and bringing them into a place where they transcend what is intrinsically Jewish and Gentile, and now constitute a *new* reality. It would be a reality never before seen, and could only be established by the power of Messiah and the glory of His life, for which He has poured out His blood and given His Spirit. Two diverse and contrary entities becoming *one* new man *is* that glory.

It is the same mystery as the mystery of marriage, in which God calls husband and wife to become one new entity in Christ *together*. The mystery is union, and union that is only made possible in the life of God in Christ. Paul's letter to the Colossians stresses the glory of the life and Ephesians speaks of the covenants and promises, but it is not God in opposition to Himself. And it is only the cross, as being the supreme demonstration of God's wisdom that makes this glory a possibility. It is the only place by which we can bring to death the things that keep us from becoming one new man, one new entity.

This mystery resembles the same kind of oneness that characterizes and describes the Trinity where three are one: the Father, Son and Holy Spirit deferring one to another in a quality of submitted relationship that inheres in being one entity. When Jew and Gentile,

---

[5] The original Greek is better translated as "the called out ones."

49

who have historically been at enmity with each other, will exhibit that same oneness, then the principalities and powers of the air will be defeated by that very demonstration. This is one of the reasons we need to pray for that remnant of Jews to be grafted back into their own root and back into the Body, in order that this mystery might be completed.

The Eternal Purpose of the Church

Paul is now going to reveal the heart of the mystery of the church and its purpose for being, particularly in relation to the principalities and powers of the air. It is the same mystery as the mystery of Israel[6] spoken of in Romans chapter 11 insofar as the fulfillment of the one is also the fulfillment of the other.

> To me, the very least of all saints, this grace was given, to preach to the Gentiles the unsearchable riches of Christ, and to bring to light what is the administration of the mystery which for ages has been hidden in God who created all things; so that the manifold wisdom of God might now be made known through the church to the rulers and the authorities in the heavenly places. This was in accordance with the eternal purpose which He carried out in Christ Jesus our Lord, in whom we have boldness and confident access through faith in Him.[7]

These scriptures hint at a primeval, cosmic conflict between light and the powers of darkness that

---

[6] See author's book *The Mystery of Israel and the Church* for a more comprehensive perspective.

[7] Ephesians 3:8-12

predates the creation of the world. There is a suggestion of a drama to be played out between two value systems: the wisdom of the gods of this world and the wisdom of God. It is a drama so enormous in God's sight that He did not think it too extravagant to create all things as a backdrop. He created the cosmos, the planets and their cycles, an earth that would be life sustaining, every species of created life, economies and civilizations. God created everything that ever was created so that it could support an entity called the church who would then have the task of bringing this conflict to its final conclusion by demonstrating, in the essence of its life, the manifold wisdom of God. He does not tell us why He wants this demonstration, but it is important to Him, and therefore we need to heed it. We are entering the last of this struggle, and I sense that the sparks will fly fiercely right until the final resolution.

There is nothing in the mindset of the world that can fit us to understand God's wisdom; it is a wisdom that is at odds with every assumed, rational and conventional understanding of life, its purpose and its meaning. Without an understanding of the purpose of the church, we will condemn church life to a mere Sunday addendum, an institutional or religious function that has ourselves and our needs as its principal purpose. We will remain fixated in time, in the immediate and visible, rooted in *our* needs, and we will never become true church until this mystery comes into the central place of our consideration. In God's genius and wisdom, He intends for us to have a view of the unseen that is calculated to free us from the bondage of narrow self-interest. He gave the church eternal purposes because He knew that if we were not occupied with something that is beyond this age, we would become so rooted *in* this present age that our witness would be ineffectual.

God's eternal purposes can only be performed through a church that demonstrates what appears to have no immediate evangelistic witness to benefit mankind. It is a cosmic demonstration, beyond the earth, and occupies *all* the ages to come. It is a demonstration that has absolutely nothing to do with *our* success, *our* well being, *our* enjoyment or with any of those things with which *we* are so occupied. It is totally irrelevant to the practicalities of our daily life, and yet our daily life will suffer in exact proportion to our indifference to the eternal purposes of God. So long as we are taken up with a myopic concentration upon ourselves and our egocentric Christianity, we will remain irrelevant in the localities God has placed us.

Too many of us have unconsciously accepted the world's definition of church, that it is an institution to serve human need. Serving human need is incidental to the greater glory:

> To Him be the glory in the church and in
> Christ Jesus to all generations forever and
> ever. Amen.[8]

God intended His glory to be normative in the church, and there was to be a radiance of this glory permeating His creation. He ordained the church to be the means by which His glory is to find entry into the earth and be made known. A church that has already opted for programs and for things that will serve the needs of men has disqualified itself from being the agency through which His purposes can be fulfilled. Mankind's greatest need, though they may not be aware of it, is to have the church make the glory of God known to them.

---

[8] Ephesians 3:21

We shall never come to kingdom righteousness so long as our needs are the predicate of our lives, the hub and pivot around which all things turn. We will never come to sanity and wholeness, nor will we ever come to the end of all our deliverance and inner-healing ministries until we recognize that our *real* sickness is our self-centeredness. To come into the eternal purposes of God will ruin us for church programs and the multitude of things we think we need in order to satisfy the congregations. The present day proliferation of programs in most churches is a statement that we have lost, or never had, the apostolic view, and like the world, we have got to provide services and benefits to hold the attention of our congregations. Let us rather be jealous for the perfect, and not lose the foundational calling of the church.

We are in an unbroken continuum with those who have embraced the purposes of God, and for which reason they were put to death, murdered and butchered in a kind of satanic fury that seeks to nullify this ultimate intention of God through those who give themselves to that purpose. That is why there are so few who want to hear the call of God, because God calls us to *His* ultimate and costly purposes.

The Wisdom of God

The wisdom of this world is predicated on self-interest, and expresses itself based on the benefit that a person receives. Mankind lives and moves and makes decisions based on how it affects *them*. A people who will give their lives for something that has no immediate, practical relevance or consequence for themselves is the wisdom of God; it is heavenly wisdom. It powerfully frees a person from self-interest. It gives him a motive for being and for doing that is outside the center in himself. The world does not believe you can do it. It wants to bring you into its vortex and have you march to its beat, with self-preservation being the law of its life. Its wisdom encourages whatever is required to preserve, advance and promote one's life. It thinks nothing of employing threats, inducements, enticements and intimidation to achieve its ends. It is the wisdom of the gods of this world, and makes mankind to fall in line and do their bidding, and to worship them as false gods.

Where there is a church that can see through the wisdom of the gods of this world, and live independently of them, and demonstrate *true* values, then those powers have no further influence whatsoever. Unless we break through to an understanding of this, our spiritual life will be stifled and church will be nothing more than a succession of services.

The Principalities and Powers of the Air

There is an invisible realm over the nations and over every locality, occupied by an order of fallen, rebellious angels, who have influenced, and continue to influence, the course of history in nations, races and men. The horrors that are taking place worldwide have their source and origin in the influence that is being exerted through men on the earth by these same powers. Mankind is unaware that they are being played upon, and through intimidation, threat, ambition, lust and fear are being enslaved and moved about by these powers.

These angelic powers were created by God and for God in order that they might administer His creation in a way that would be conducive to His purpose in mankind's coming to the knowledge of Him. They were created to preserve a certain structure to God's creation in order that man might seek and find Him. However, in their rebellion, they are usurping the role and office that was given them, and are turning the attention of men away from God. When this administrative order fell, it took on the spirit of Satan who wanted to rise above the Most High. This is an ultimate egotism. Not content to serve the purposes of God administratively, they have used that place to win the allegiance, loyalty, devotion and worship of men unto themselves. They are fallen and defeated powers, yet they can still influence, corrupt and adversely affect entire societies, communities and nations, even operating through the institutions of religion, commerce, politics and culture.

This cosmic context ought to be foundational in the consciousness of the church, without which we condemn ourselves to an essentially futile Christianity.

> Our struggle is not against flesh and blood,
> but against the rulers, against the powers,
> against the world forces of this darkness,
> against the spiritual forces of wickedness in
> the heavenly places.[9]

We wrestle; this is a collective and corporate requirement of a church that has come to that place of true corporateness. That is why Satan would much rather see us doing all of our good deeds and individual activities, so that we are kept from obtaining the place by which we can come to such a composite character *together*.

---

[9] Ephesians 6:12

The Two Wisdoms

The church is called to a cosmic struggle in a battle with the powers of darkness over the whole issue of which wisdom will prevail over God's creation. Wisdom does not mean what we would ordinarily think it to mean; it is not wise sayings, but more like a value system. The wisdom of the gods of this world is a system predicated on influencing men to preserve themselves and to make their own survival the first law of life. Their system is the unchallenged premise by which the world lives its life, namely, the avoidance of pain and the pursuit of pleasure, and makes *this* the foremost purpose of its being. The ability to lay down one's life and not to consider that one's life is dear to oneself[10] is the wisdom of God.

God's wisdom is predicated on weakness and foolishness. The one wisdom lives for itself, its own preservation and its own advantages, while God's wisdom lives for another. The wisdom of the Son of God is selfless; He never initiated anything for Himself, but lived entirely for the gratification of His Father. This is the wisdom that the world cannot bear. The only one who can live like that truly is one who does not think that this life is the whole story. There is an eternity, and it is the true appreciation of eternity that enables us to be fearless in this life. If we suffer the loss of our life, we are fully persuaded that it is not mere happenstance or accident, but ordained of God, and that there will be a reward for that sacrifice and suffering. God's wisdom is to relinquish, to give up, to yield and to believe that there is something greater than death and, by that, to overcome the fear of death.

---

[10] See Revelation 12:11

Defeating the Powers

When we are ourselves insecure, fearful, guarding our lives, afraid to take the risks of faith and playing it safe, then the powers of the air are not required to acknowledge us at all. They are only impressed with the same thing they saw both in Jesus and in Paul, namely, apostolic authenticity, the reality of God Himself. They are required to recognize only that which is of God and like God, as authentic as He Himself is. God is wanting authenticity in His people; He is wanting heavenliness, truth, unfeigned love and all the true values that are so painful to obtain. We have all been the products of a superficial and devious civilization that majors on appearances and outward things. Where the powers of the air see the truth of God in the life of His people, they will retreat. They know whom to fear and whom to acknowledge.[11]

We can turn up our worship amplifiers as much as we want, we can shout down the powers as much as we want, but I suspect they merely sit back and yawn. It is not noise that impresses them, but character. It is the truth of our lives where we really live, not the brave show that we put on in front of others. They are required to flee when they see in our conduct and character the visible evidence of our freedom from the influence of their wisdom, freedom from fear, freedom from being intimidated.

The wisdom of God was superbly demonstrated at the cross of Calvary when the supreme Son of God relinquished the right to His own life, and gave it up by the eternal Spirit, the Spirit of sacrifice, without spot and without blemish to the Father. He offered Himself up without complaint and without answering His

---

[11] See Acts 19:15

critics back; He did not respond in kind. He was a Lamb who went silently to the slaughter. He was goaded and mocked by His own people to come down from the cross before they would believe Him. He suffered that anguish for others while at the same time hearing their taunts and jibes. If there was anything in Him that had to do with self-justification and self-vindication, it would have welled up in indignation under the extremity of that crisis. But instead He says, "Father, forgive them; for they do not know what they are doing."[12] Another wisdom was expressed contrary to the logic which that moment would have justified. Jesus fully absorbed the fury of the powers of darkness that wanted to destroy Him, thus obliterating the threat that He represented to their kingdom.

> When He had disarmed the rulers and authorities, He made a public display of them, having triumphed over them through Him.[13]

By demonstrating the superior wisdom of God at the cross, Jesus disarmed and brought a foundational and devastating setback to the principalities and powers. The powers of the air exhibited their wisdom of threat, intimidation and the use of force to get Him to react by railing against those who were railing against Him. Jesus consistently demonstrated the wisdom of God by silently bearing the worst that they could inflict. Wisdom is not something that is necessarily vocally exhibited; it has got to be demonstrated in life. Ultimate malignity met ultimate magnanimity; evil met the ultimate graciousness of God, the forbearance of God, the humility of God and the forgiveness of God. Meekness triumphed over

---

[12] Luke 23:34a
[13] Colossians 2:15

viciousness, and it is the same demonstration that will make God eternally joyous, but this time through the church, for which reason He has created all things.

The powers thought that they had won because they had brought Jesus into death, but He bore that death in a way that revealed the wisdom of God; and it is *this* which defeats them. If they cannot manipulate you to be like them and protect your carnal and bodily life and cry out and compromise and do anything just to stay alive, then they have no more power over you. If you are willing to die in your integrity in the faith, and count that as privilege, what more can they do to defeat you? You have defeated them because the worst that they can do has come upon you, and you have stood and remained faithful to God, and exhibited the character of God in your suffering.

> Yet we do speak wisdom among those who are mature; a wisdom, however, not of this age nor of the rulers of this age, who are passing away; but we speak God's wisdom in a mystery, the hidden wisdom which God predestined before the ages to our glory; the wisdom which none of the rulers of this age has understood; for if they had understood it they would not have crucified the Lord of glory.[14]

By imposing a wisdom predicated upon force and destruction, they did not realize that they were releasing a resurrection and a life that would billow out over mankind throughout all generations, and would bring the final triumph of God and the raising of the dead. It set in motion the very things that would establish His throne in the very city where He was put to death. Through His death and out of His rent side, a

---

[14] Colossians 2:6-8

predominantly Gentile body of believers would be birthed. The Holy Spirit would be poured out from the throne of God, thus giving an enablement and a power to fulfill the Gentile mandate and commission of ushering in His own millennial glory and kingdom upon the throne of David. The powers suffered a severe setback with the crucifixion of Jesus when He made an open spoil of them, and took the keys of death and of Hell from them. He disarmed them, but He did not inflict the final defeat. Their final defeat remains to be fulfilled by the church in the mystery of God.

A Corporate Demonstration

We are coming to the end of the age, and the magnitude of the eternal purposes of God requires a demonstration of a corporate kind. We are in something together, both the minister and the housewife, and we need to prepare ourselves for the final conclusion of this mystery. It requires a people freed from the influence of the principalities and the powers of the air. It requires a people who are not living for themselves. It requires a people who are gloriously free from the love of money; who are indifferent to shopping malls, and who can receive the stripping of their earthly goods with joy, knowing that they have a better possession and a lasting one.[15] They are those who can suffer afflictions and inexplicable circumstances without becoming undone.

In fact, the only people who can fulfill this mystery are those who would be "strangers and exiles on the earth."[16] They have risen above and beyond their national culture. They know that their security is

---

[15] See Hebrews 10:34
[16] See Hebrews 11:13

not from the Government, or their employer, but from God. If that source should dry up, then the Lord has alternative sources.

Elsewhere in the scriptures we read of the reward that the Lord gives to faithful stewards. In the millennial age to come, some will rule over two cities, some over five and some over ten. The millennium is the advent and establishment of God's eternal rule on the earth. It is a theocratic kingdom administered through glorified saints in the heavenlies, overcomers in this life, who will have different places in the rule of God, and the reward of God, according to their fruitfulness in this life. Once this life is finished, those issues are decided. It is not sinful to be jealous for eternal distinction and reward; it is something that ought to be in our present consciousness and desire. Do we have works that will survive the fires of the judgment seat of Christ? Are we laying up treasure in heaven? Are we heavenly-minded? Are we eternally-minded? Are we millennially-minded?

With this mindset, we will find we have come to a new kind of contempt for the things that are visible, temporal and seen. Like Paul, we will find ourselves enjoying and contemplating the things that are invisible and eternal. By the eye of the Spirit, we will see the eternal weight of glory that makes the things in this life momentary and our sufferings as light affliction. Paul did not focus on the things that were visible, the things that we love to set our eyes upon. If this world, its wisdom, its morality, its perversions and its corruption do not daily chafe us, then the world is too much with us. We need to be chafed, as righteous Lot was, and to be constantly praying, "Come, Lord Jesus!"

Chapter 6

Apostolic Lifestyle

The church's call to an authentic poverty of lifestyle is not an option we can lightly dismiss. Religiously speaking, we can make a performance out of it, and thereby cheapen it through an induced poverty and abstinence. By so doing, we would be making a humanly contrived substitute that will achieve nothing in the kingdom of God. However, there is a valid place for simplicity of lifestyle and dependency upon God.

> Know this first of all, that in the last days mockers will come with their mocking, following after their own lusts, and saying, "Where is the promise of His coming? For ever since the fathers fell asleep, all continues just as it was from the beginning of creation."[1]

---

[1] 2 Peter 3:3-4

Peter writes about believers in the last days who will mock and scoff, because they have no anticipation of the Lord's coming. Their view of the faith and their expectation of His coming will have been corrupted by their lusts and evil desires.

The Lord's coming is a vital doctrine, one that is at the heart of the gospel. To mock or scoff at His coming is to mock the faith and the word of God itself. Mocking is a scornful attitude, and we can mock by something that is not necessarily expressed in our words, but just by the way we conduct ourselves. For example, making careful and meticulous provision for our retirement, or looking forward to a long life, is effectually scoffing against the known doctrine of the coming of the Lord. Another example would be church groups and denominations actively seeking to perpetuate their own institutions, making every kind of provision for the future, but essentially acting as if He is *not* coming.

By the same token, the erecting of multi-million dollar church buildings is not the statement of a people who are looking toward a soon-coming end, a Lord who is "at the door," and who is coming with last days' devastations and judgments. We will not be able to enjoy our sumptuous architectural monstrosities or glass palaces then. More than we know, our building programs do testify that we are not actually looking for His coming, but if one were to suggest to the authorities of that fellowship that that is scoffing, they would be aghast, because they *subscribe* to the doctrine of the Lord's coming, but only as a *doctrine*.

There is a difference between holding a doctrine and having an existential expectation. It is not the mere holding of doctrines that distinguishes us as the church, but rather, do we have an actual, apocalyptic expectation of an end? Is the end of the age such a pulsating reality for us that our plans for our retirement are radically affected? The use of our money and time is directly related to what we believe with regard to a soon-coming end, and if our conduct in our use of time and money contradict the doctrine of the Lord's coming, then we are effectually scoffing.

In the early church, those who had houses and land sold them, and laid the proceeds at the feet of the apostles. They thought, "I do not need this. The Lord is at the door. The end is near. Why am I clutching my possessions? I will make my goods available now so that the poor amongst us might not have need." They had an apocalyptic expectancy that the end was near, and lived in this anticipation as being the logical outworking of their faith.

More than we know, our theological positions are regulated by our needs and desires for the gratification of our bodily lusts. We may not be conscious of it, but if we were to examine the moral condition of our lives, we would find out why it is that we have so little faith. Lust has an enormous power to dull the mind and spirit to the truths of God. A lust is by nature a desire, and there is a world of difference between a legitimate desire or need compared to a desire that God looks upon as a lust that will affect our theological and doctrinal expectations.

A legitimate desire has its origin in God. The fact that it is permissible to drink soda pop all you want, even before breakfast, does *not* make it godly. Just because it is freely available does not legitimize that desire. Though it may seem innocent in itself, that kind of indulgence opens the way for other things, the full and final outcome of which is to dull our hearts toward the things of God. Do we submit our desires before the Lord? Is He the Lord of the things we think small and insignificant, particularly in this merchandising world? There is a whole realm of things pertaining to lifestyle that have been made legitimate in our minds because of their availability, but there will be negative spiritual consequences on a lifestyle that panders to those lusts. We need to be free from a self-gratifying lifestyle that the world would impose upon us and convince us that it is legitimate and normal, but which is contrary in every point to self-denial.

In Egypt, I once watched brothers traveling with me become wretched if they did not get their hamburgers and French-fries. They could not go on without the savory sensation of grilled meat and greasy fries sliding over their taste buds. The same could be said for those who continually have a coffee cup in their hand. Any dependency, even though it is not in itself intrinsically evil, needs to be watched. This is not being legalistic; rather, it is sounding an alert, because lust has an incredible power, and that is what the apostle Peter is describing. I love ice cream, but I have observed that indulging in it does something to my sensuality. That is why fasting is so powerful because the stomach needs to be reminded who is in charge.

The apostle Paul kept his body under subjection, continually buffeting it in one form or another.

> Therefore I run in such a way, as not without aim; I box in such a way, as not beating the air; but I discipline my body and make it my slave, so that, after I have preached to others, I myself will not be disqualified.[2]

For Paul, it constituted an actual warfare, lest, having preached to others, he would be disqualified,

---

[2] 1 Corinthians 9:26-27

meaning that he did not want to be disqualified from the eternal reward and distinctions of sonship, or to be cast away from the privilege of millennial blessedness because of an indulgence in his body. That is why this same man, when he was stripped, brutally beaten and thrown into an inner dungeon, could "pray and sing hymns of praise to God."[3] His physical body was not the focus of his life.

Overweight ministers are an embarrassment to the faith. For me, their credibility is immediately lessened because they are not keeping their bodies under subjection. What then of their spirits? How seriously can they be taken? How seriously should the unsaved world take them, especially when they see believers compromised by the same lusts that they have? If you do not recognize that you have given yourself over to some habit forming thing, try doing away with it for the rest of the week and see if there is not some clamor coming up from inside that demands gratification.

> For many walk, of whom I often told you, and now tell you even weeping, that they are enemies of the cross of Christ, whose end is destruction, whose god is their appetite, and whose glory is in their shame, who set their minds on earthly things.[4]

Paul specifically mentions those who have turned away from the cross and have made their stomach's appetite their god. We live in the world of merchandising, but there is rejoicing in heaven when Babylon comes down in one hour.[5] The merchants, who have made their riches by it, lament and mourn. Babylon is not formed at some future time, but is

---

[3] See Acts 16:22-25
[4] Philippians 3:18-19
[5] See Revelation chapter 18

already with us, and if we cannot get our "fix," then we will find ourselves taking the number of the Beast in order to obtain it. Are we able to live with a simple diet? Or will we take the number so that we can buy and sell and get the things that we think we *must* have? Esau thought that the loss of a bowl of lentils was going to be his death. He was so habituated to his stomach and the gratification of his bodily lusts that he sold his birthright for that most base satisfaction.

We had a discussion once in the community about "Sugar Pops" breakfast cereal. It went on for hours, and you would not believe the vehemence of that discussion over what kind of cereal was appropriate for our end-time community, and especially for our children. It is amazing what is revealed when the Lord takes the lid off, which can only happen in community, because if you live privately, who is going to concern themselves with what kind of cereal to buy? It was revealed that if our kids were not placated in what they wanted, then they made their mothers uncomfortably agitated and rattled during the day. Eventually, it affected the sex life of the husband, and *this* was the real issue! The husband had to face the problem of sexual denial because the wife was in a restless condition, for which reason he was most insistent that his kids could have whatever cereal they wanted.

We began to see the naked rebellion that lies underneath the surface of God's people, and it would not have been revealed unless the issue of our children's cereal had come up. We would never have known it if we continued to buy and eat what we wanted. It became an issue when it was too expensive to buy those cereals, and we saw how much cheaper it was to buy bulk quantities of grain, and out of that crisis came the revelation of what I have just described.

When a woman, who loved the message of the cross, came to us from California and could not get her orange juice, she actually lied to obtain a supply. She hid it, like Ananias and Sapphira. When the cross touched the issue of her orange juice, something of an evil kind was revealed in her heart that she may well have carried into eternity had she remained in California. We talked about it in our prayer time, "Well, if it was vitamin C tablets, would you have lied to obtain some?" No, because the issue was not vitamin C; it was the gratification of the taste and enjoyment of orange juice; she *had* to have it. It was not the issue of nutrition, but the issue of lust and gratification through something that is made delightful in its taste. It was a revelation of what we will do to gratify ourselves over flavor, even to lie and to contradict the cross! Whether it was orange juice for one woman, or a hamburger, or ice cream, or cereal for another, the Lord showed us that every one of us had to have our "fix," and it was compromising us all.

Food and drink have a powerful, magnetic and seductive draw, and the sensation of taste, the holding of it in the mouth and allowing the thing to slide down the throat, all indicate that our desire for it can go far beyond the issue of nutrition. There is a component to food, though created by God, that is played upon by those who benefit and profit themselves at our expense through delight and sense-experience. We can go on to a whole dissertation, not only about food, but also about clothing, cars, and indeed, the entire lifestyle that we have allowed to settle upon us, contrary to the character of the kingdom of God and His righteousness.

When establishing the community, even the kind of housing we should put up became an issue. Were we to be some kind of retirement community, living in the woods in nice, rustic, middle-class housing, or was our lifestyle to be proportionate to our message? If we were to minister in a poverty stricken country, how credible would our word be and how much authority would we have? The preached word is altogether related to our lifestyle, and lifestyle will affect the quality, the authority, the intensity and the power of our preached word. In establishing our households, the question arose of how much living space we needed. How many square feet was appropriate? Our western society has established a certain mode of life that is not necessarily God's standard. We found that it was only in coming into a community situation that the things reinforcing our selfishness are found out. But, in being found out, we are broken up and released for the kind of magnanimity, generosity and fellowship that was the distinctive genius of the early church.

The Intensification of Life

In community, the complexities of life are compounded more furiously and over a shorter period of time. There is no how-to manual for community living, and God intends that no such manual should exist. If we could prescribe a way of doing it, then it would no longer be the kingdom of God, but *our* kingdom. How the kingdom is to be expressed has to be given in the locality where we are, according to the design of God Himself, distinctive and appropriate to the situation we are in. We do not have to be governed or ruled by earthly factors like employment or location. There are unquestioned premises by which the world itself operates, for example, the forty-hour work week and the necessity for a certain standard of living or lifestyle. These things need to be radically examined and altered in the light of the kingdom of God, and in what the Lord is expressly requiring, though it contradicts the conventional pattern. For instance, would we be willing to work shorter hours, or for less pay, if it meant that the purposes of God could be advanced?

We are instructed in the scriptures to seek first His kingdom and His righteousness.[6] How many of us in fact do it? In seeking first His kingdom, and in putting the values of the kingdom *before* the values of our employment, or the things that our employment makes possible, we may well find ourselves facing many changes. No one is compelling us to live by what we are able to earn in the world. What are the values that are closest to our hearts? Is it the suburban retreat, or the home that we have loved for years, or do we want the proximity with the brethren, for which we are willing to forsake *that* pleasure, however dear and however long we may have enjoyed it? This is part of what it means to seek first the kingdom of God. We should not be mindlessly saddled by the world's pattern, but rather invite the light of the kingdom into our present situation. Are our lifestyles, employment and the use of our money and time consonant with the kingdom of God?

We need to have a revelation of the deep egocentric orientation of modern Christianity, and how it affects and afflicts us all, and to recognize how Herculean a power is needed to break that centrifugal force, releasing our lives to be spent for God. Our motives need constantly to be examined in the interaction with the brethren on an intensive daily basis where nothing can be concealed, and where the light of God can be brought into the things that are hidden. To

[6] See Matthew 6:33

begin to see ourselves as God sees us is one of the virtues of community itself. The early apostles had the daily interaction, and we need to desire its restoration.

Someone always comes up to me and says, "But Art, I live too far away. My job means that I cannot be in close fellowship as often as you are suggesting. What should I do?" I reply, "Sell your house and move closer. Change your job. Work fewer hours. Lower your standard of living. Give up your luxuries. Live more simply. Do not give all that time to the world. Make time for the people of God." Are we willing to give up our middle-class homes of comfort and privacy in order to come into a place of proximity with each other? The loss of comfort, privacy and convenience are the sufferings of the cross, but where are our values anyway? The world encourages us to have a privatistic lifestyle, and our co-operation with the world is reflected in the way in which we ourselves love our privacy. We do not want it interrupted, but something has got to be sacrificed, and, as with everything else, it comes down to the issue of the cross.

Chapter 7

Fellowship and the Mystery of the Trinity

> What was from the beginning, what we
> have heard, what we have seen with our
> eyes, what we have looked at and touched
> with our hands, concerning the Word of
> Life; and the life was manifested, and we
> have seen and testify and proclaim to you
> the eternal life, which was with the Father
> and was manifested to us; what we have
> seen and heard we proclaim to you also, so
> that you too may have fellowship with us;
> and indeed our fellowship is with the
> Father, and with His Son Jesus Christ.[1]

The same phrase, "In the beginning, God…" is
also used in Genesis chapter one, so it would seem that
John is consciously trying to parallel the first words of
Genesis to show an arc of continuity with the whole

---

[1] 1 John 1:1-3

flow of God's redemptive drama in history. God is the Alpha and the Omega, the beginning and the end. In an almost jarring combination of terms, John speaks of the distant past, and then, in the very same verse, he talks about every day things such as "touching with our hands." It is almost like the paradox of heaven and earth being brought together in one statement. Touching and handling divinity in that manner sounds disrespectful, but what is John's purpose in using earthly references such as touching and seeing in the same breath with the eternality of the One who was being described? The bringing together of disparate things, which seemingly contradict one another, becomes all the more compelling, and for that reason, we should rightly give it our full attention.

The environment in which this epistle was written will give us a key to why John is emphasizing the tangible, physical and visible. He is addressing readers who were in a state of confusion over certain prevalent ideas and moods that were affecting Jewish and non-Jewish believers in that part of the world. He is addressing a controversy that was already pervading the church at that time, namely, the dismissal of the incarnate reality of Jesus. "How do you fit Deity into a body?" one might have questioned.

The Principle of Incarnation

In fact, God coming in the flesh may well be at the heart of *every* opposition to God. It is certainly an offense to Jews, both presently and historically, but there is a degree in which it is just as much an offense to the church in this day and age. Many will acknowledge God's coming in the flesh theologically and ideologically, and they will acknowledge that this

73

was true of Jesus historically; but they will not acknowledge anything more than that. If you go beyond that, and say that God is in *your* flesh, or in flesh that we know or see, the whole offense of incarnation is raised again. Though we may agree that God was in the flesh of Jesus, have we really made our peace with the radical implication of the doctrine? We might be only condescending to what we know technically to be true, and therefore indisputable, but have we really been brought into the ultimate mystery of incarnation, namely, God in *man*? If we have not, it will surface, and show itself in one form or another. Our agreement with acceptable doctrine does not necessarily make it true agreement. To merely nod our heads benignly and acknowledge that, yes, God came in the flesh, and then move on, is not really dealing with how staggering a thing Jesus represented in His coming, and how staggering a thing it still is.

It was not beneath the dignity of God to be confined to human form. Jesus would have needed to defecate, urinate, sweat and go through the humiliating things that we all go through. How many of us have not been humiliated with a bowel movement? Let us turn the clock back, and let us say that Jesus walked into the room with the words, "If you see Me, you see the Father; I and the Father are one," and we are looking at this guy and thinking, "Is that sweat I see on His brow? Do I sense a little bodily exhaustion there?" Do we understand how *any* man coming and purporting to be *one with God* would stagger us? There are reasons why God came in bodily form, but we need to really understand the essence of the offense, because it does not end with Jesus.

The principle of incarnation should be at the very heart and vitality of church life. If we are offended by the glory of that reality, we effectually block the phenomenon from being the present principle of our own life. No one wants to say, "If you hear me, you are hearing the words of God." Paul makes that astounding statement, "For me, to live is Christ," and we say, "Well, that is okay for Paul, but no-one from our generation should dare presume to be in the kind of relationship that Paul had with Jesus, and that Jesus had with the Father." By thinking such things, we are *not* apprehending the dynamic that God intends as normative for the church; we are satisfying ourselves with mere technical agreement, and the mystery of this glory will not be our experience. Unless we have the same relationship with God that Paul had, we ourselves will be falling short of the glory of God.

In His own incarnation, God's definitive intention was to set before us the very model that we are called to exemplify. Now *that* is the good news! The gospel of God is much greater than the issue of forgiveness of sins. The *life* that was made manifest is now available and accessible to those who have the faith to appropriate it, and who have yielded to the condition for the giving of that life.

By forgiving men their sins, by taking on the prerogatives of God, by allowing men to worship Him, Jesus made extravagant claims about who He was. What then was the incontrovertible proof of the truth of His statements? What demonstrable evidence did He give that required men to acknowledge Him as God? John's answer is that "the Life was manifested." In other words, *God* was manifested. But what did Jesus manifest to Israel that would make His claims as "God in the flesh" valid? What was the manifestation of that life? How would those who lived with Him answer that question, those who touched, felt and looked upon Him? As moderns, we have texts, commentaries and a whole corpus of understanding,

75

but what was the basis for *John's* affirmation that the life was made manifest? We know that Jesus manifested the *character* of God, but is John alluding to character alone? It is true that suffering unto death reveals most profoundly the truth of the character of anyone, but *before* Jesus' crucifixion, men were bowing and calling Him, "My Lord and My God." John would have said that the life was manifested before the crucifixion, and I am asking, "Where and how?"

Why was Nicodemus not bowled over in his conversation with Jesus? The life was manifest before him, but he came away from that encounter bewildered and confused. What would *we* expect to see manifested if God were to take upon Himself the form of flesh and dwell among us? God is the Creator, God is righteousness, God is glory, God is power and God is holiness. God is beyond definition, and yet, He comes in the flesh and manifests Himself in a human body. What would that manifestation take, so that we could agree that this is God?

If those to whom He came had erroneous views about God, projections of their own imagining, they would have been disappointed by what Jesus manifested. They would not expect God to be manifesting humility and meekness. They would expect God to come with "real" credentials, and "real" authority, letting everyone know that this was very God. Yet God was not manifested according to the stereotypical expectations of a generation that was far removed from Him. They expected a Deliverer who would expel the Romans and restore the glory of Israel. But here is this unobtrusive character, having no place to lay His head, an itinerant preacher coming from a city of low reputation, and yet, John says that He manifested the life! What therefore is the essence of that life? What is the unmistakable and essential constitution of the life of God, even when it is expressed through a sweating man? What inescapable trademark, character and quality must that life express? Will everyone who has opportunity to glimpse it be persuaded it is the life of God?

In the beginning God said, "Let there be light, and there was light," and if that same God is manifested in human form at a later time, whatever will be said ought to bear some resonance of the God who said, "Let there be light." When He says to a fisherman, or to a tax collector, "Follow Me," the man gets up from his table and vocation, and follows Him. A word came of the same resonance, quality and authority that spoke to the chaos and said, "Let there be…and there was."

Since God is the word, one of the most important manifestations of the life would therefore be the word that issues from the one who purports to be of God, with God, and indeed, God Himself, and it is evidenced in just two words, "Follow Me." Men got up and did just that. They were not hypnotized; they heard something, and a disposition in their heart of a reverence toward God responded.

Many were offended and turned away, but when Jesus asked His disciples whether they too would turn away, Peter replied, "Lord, to whom shall we go? You have words of eternal life."[2] They might just as well have said, "You *are* the words of eternal life; the words that proceed from You are the unequivocal demonstration of that truth." The word of God is life, and it will either be received as life, or, being rejected as life, it will bring death; it will bring a hardening, "If you hear His voice, do not harden your hearts."[3] There

---

[2] See John 6:68
[3] See Hebrews 3:7,8 and 15

is no room for neutrality here. God cannot be present without something taking place, as was evidenced in the entire earthly ministry of Jesus.

The Fellowship as Incarnation

The summation of all they had seen, heard, known and experienced testified that this was *the* life. It was not just an isolated expression here or there, but the totality, including the character, that was displayed. And now, the mystery is that Christian fellowship is called to be the incarnation of that same reality:

> What we have seen and heard we proclaim to you also, so that you too may have fellowship with us; and indeed our fellowship is with the Father, and with His Son Jesus Christ.[4]

The divine logic is that the life was manifested, and it is on the basis of this life that you will have fellowship. In other words, fellowship ought to be the expression of the same reality that was manifest in Jesus. Now *your* earthly body has God in its midst, or you could not have fellowship. Fellowship is not a social club that can be performed on the basis of politeness or human camaraderie. This is ultimate relationship, known only to the Trinity. The mystery is that this life is going to be made manifest in the earth, and it will be the same quality of fellowship, because now we have the key to the enablement, namely, the life that was made manifest. And if we do not have the life, we are making a phony profession; we have only a principle, not the reality.

---

[4] 1 John 1:3

God added to the weight of things by bringing Gentiles into the picture. If it had only been Jews, they could have continued like the Pharisees, an exclusive club. However, with all the differences represented in Jew and Gentile, including the ages-long enmity that exists, this same quality of relationship was expected to be found in them, together, as one new entity; and it can only be made possible through the *life* of God, which, as we shall see, is the *love* of God. In this, we can see the genius of God in opening the doors to Gentiles in order to save the early Jewish converts from the kind of presumption toward which they were already tending.

True fellowship is the continuation of the mystery of the Godhead, now made up of both Jews and Gentiles. This is the most extraordinary fellowship ever in the history of mankind. Fellowship is not fellowship until we are in the light as He is in the light, and we will know we are in this actuality because *joy* will attest to it, "These things we write, so that our joy may be made complete."[5] Joy will issue naturally and spontaneously when we are in the reality of the kind of fellowship that the Godhead enjoys together.

> They went out from us, but they were not really of us; for if they had been of us, they would have remained with us; but they went out, so that it would be shown that they all are not of us.[6]

Why would anyone want to leave this kind of fellowship? Are we hoping to find a more perfect form of fellowship than the one we have left? That itself is error, because we are not going to find a more perfect form; we are going to find other believers

---

[5] Ibid., v.4
[6] 1 John 2:19

going through the same kinds of struggles. To leave one group of believers in order to find a more ideal alternative is an indication that we do not understand what true fellowship is. It reveals that we are unwilling to face the constituent elements of true fellowship. And that is why John can emphatically dismiss these people; their very going out was the statement in itself, or else they would have remained. There was no reason to go out if they were the people of God, but the fact that they have gone out indicates that they were not what they purported to be. You can no more go out from fellowship than you can go out from the Lord, who has the words of eternal life. Where else shall we go? We cannot go out from a true expression of that and still purport to have a relationship with God.

The joy of the Lord can only be full in *that* quality of relationship and reality. There can be a constant sea of joy that is not always felt or experienced as delight. Joy is a solid undergirding that enables us to bear the friction, tensions and momentary differences that will, in time, be reconciled, and we can wait for that time without coming apart at the seams, or looking at the brother as an enemy or a threat. We can bear the things that God is working out, and though it may not be pleasant at the time, there is a joy that enables us to patiently bear.

> The one who loves His brother abides in the Light and there is no cause for stumbling in him. But the one who hates his brother is in the darkness and walks in the darkness, and does not know where he is going because the darkness has blinded his eyes.[7]

---

[7] 1 John 2:10-11

John connects abiding in the light to the issue of love. What is the quality of our love for the most difficult, threatening or irritating brother? The issue of light is also the issue of clarity of seeing, not only in relationship, but in all areas of life, so that there is no prospect of stumbling in one who loves. John, guided by the Spirit to express the wisdom of God, equates love with the issue of light; and light is essential to right walking.

This group who had left John's fellowship continued to announce themselves as Christians, and even raised aspersions as to whether John was the real thing and his fellowship authentic!

> By this we know that we have come to know Him, if we keep His commandments.[8]

For John, the evidence of a real knowing of God is expressed by obedience to the commandments, the most difficult and impossible of all being to love the brethren. You can only obey it because you are *in* Him who is love, and that is how you can distinguish those who make phony professions of the knowledge of God from those who are actually *in* the true faith. The word "in" is everywhere used throughout the text. This is the controversy, and John's letter is to reassure those in the faith who are being questioned concerning what they represent.

> The one who says, "I have come to know Him," and does not keep His commandments, is a liar, and the truth is not in him.[9]

If we have no intention of obeying this commandment, then that is already the evidence we are only making a fraudulent, verbal profession of the

---

[8] 1 John 2:3
[9] 1 John 2:4

faith. A sincere believer would desire to honor the God who has given the commandment, though he knows it is impossible to fulfill out of his own unaided humanity.

> But whoever keeps His word, in him the love of God has truly been perfected. By this we know that we are in Him.[10]

The completion of love is a process that comes through obedience. This is how we know we are in Him. This is the undeniable evidence of the truth of one's claim to be *in* Christ, namely, our obedience to the commandment. The phrase, "has truly been perfected" indicates that this kind of perfection is not automatic, nor is it all there from the beginning of our Christian walk.

The standard is a love higher than the love you have for someone who is like you; even the Pharisees could do that. If we could only understand how different the God of love and the love of God are from anything that we understand as love. This is the new and high standard raised by the demonstration of Jesus' love for sinners, and it is *this* standard that God now seeks to be exemplified in the fellowship by the same sacrificial extension of the love of the brethren one for another. In fact, we cannot understand love unless we understand what God demonstrated through Jesus at the cross; He bore the wrath of the Father, that men need not suffer the wrath of God while they are yet sinners. Love takes on a new meaning, and then becomes the standard for true fellowship. But if we miss what is represented at the cross, we lose the standard, and our "love" can be no more than a sentimental feeling or an affectionate emotion.

---

[10] Ibid., v.5

> The one who says he abides in Him ought
> himself to walk in the same manner as He
> walked.[11]

We have again the powerful emphasis on incarnation. In other words, if we are *in* Him, then the God who is love continually finds expression through us in the same manner that it was expressed through Jesus in His own body. Incarnation is a "believing *into* Him" and an abiding out of that place. This is the only basis upon which God's standard can be met. Only God can obey His own commandments, which is why we are called to an *ultimate* obedience, drawing from an ultimate source, from the God who is love in Himself.

The love of God *is* God, and unless it is wrought in us, or we are *in* Him who is love, what then can we demonstrate? Even to think that we can produce something that looks like love, because it is emotional or affectionate, is an effectual denial of God. And the truth of this can only be tested in the authenticity of fellowship itself, where the self-generated love will collapse. In the intensity of life, abrasive things will always come to the surface. There are too many points of disagreement among believers for it to be otherwise. And the only way you can work through the tensions and trials is by the love of God, by seeking to obey the commandment. And, as you seek, God's love is made complete. Therefore, we must earnestly desire to be *in* Christ in order that His love might be given to us.

The love that characterizes relationships of those who are outside of Christ is a self-gratifying love that seeks to possess another person for one's own gratification; it looks for gratification in an object that it deems worthy of affection and attention. God's love

---

[11] Ibid., v.6

is a self-sacrificial yielding, in which you expect no benefit from extending yourself. This is exactly what Jesus did at the cross, and only that kind of love is capable of extending itself for the unlovely. God's love does not depend upon the object of its love being worthy or deserving, but wholly upon what God is in Himself.

True Fellowship

> We are from God; he who knows God listens to us; he who is not from God does not listen to us. By this we know the spirit of truth and the spirit of error.[12]

It sounds like John is presuming to make himself and those joined with him as being the standard of proof itself; so that if you will not hear John, you are evidently out of the faith and in error. Anyone who dares speak like this today would likely be considered a heretic. Is John exhibiting love? If this is really true, John's words must therefore be an expression of the love of God, despite the likelihood of being misconstrued.

> No one has seen God at any time; if we love one another, God abides in us, and His love is perfected in us. By this we know that we abide in Him and He in us, because He has given us of His Spirit.[13]

This is incarnational theology centering in the life of God, the life that we have seen, that we have handled, the eternal life. If we are in the life, we will express the love. Both the desire to obey the

---

[12] 1 John 4:6
[13] 1 John 4:12-13

commandment and the enablement to obey are themselves the expression of that life. In modern times, the tendency of the church is to dismiss this union as only a mode of speaking, and therefore to miss its literalness. There is a real "in Him," and in the life, and in the love, all of which have to have their outworking in the fellowship.

> There is no fear in love; but perfect love casts out fear, because fear involves punishment, and the one who fears is not perfected in love.[14]

Fear inhibits the expression of love. Love makes us vulnerable by opening us to painful things, to disappointments and misrepresentations. Guarding ourselves from that possibility is a sign of fear. Fear restricts and prevents the love from being made perfect and complete. Fear inhibits love, and that may be the single greatest factor for the lack of evidence of the love of God. Our own fear of being rejected makes us defensive and afraid, and therefore keeps love from being made complete. The practical outworking of fear in a fellowship is the fear of opening ourselves to love, which is a symptom of the larger fear and insecurity concerning our eternal destiny. But if we had *that* confidence, we would be freer to open ourselves to the realities of love.

Truly being "in Him" finds its nourishment in true fellowship. Eating and drinking at the Lord's Table is the renewing of the covenantal relationship with His life. In covenant, He has given His life for our rags; *this* is the good news. It is not just the forgiveness of sins, but the giving of the life and love of God in exchange for our threadbare and inadequate human substitute. Every time we take the covenantal cup, we

---

[14] Ibid., v.18

are reaffirming this precious gift. The early Eastern Orthodox church, which historically is thought to have its origins from John the apostle, was very incarnationally-minded, with a great emphasis on communion and being in the life. Our modern church life has drifted away from that, and is much more credal and cerebral in its doctrines and categories; we approve the doctrines, but we are not necessarily in the life of which the doctrines speak.

Love will issue from being in the life, and if it takes forms we do not recognize, we should not be offended. The God who is love must give the form of the love; we must let love have its every expression. The only thing that keeps this incarnational theology from becoming esoteric mysticism is the down-to-earth necessity for the love of the brethren: "The one who loves God should love His brother also."[15] God always brings us back to the stubborn reality of relational love with the brethren. He never allows love to be carried away into a hermit kind of isolated existence, but instead brings it into the grit and reality of actual love to the brethren in all of their diversity.

Incarnational ground is holy ground; it is at the very heart of the genius of true fellowship and the mode of being God intended as normative for His people. This is the glory of the faith. If we would rather perfect our own righteousness out of our humanity or religiosity instead of drawing from the life, then we are outside the faith.

To what degree does the Son have *us*? Are we totally yielded to the Son that He would *be* our life? Or are we living independently of Him? Is His life real and sufficient for our love, wisdom, truth and righteousness? Are we casting ourselves totally and

---

[15] 1 John 4:21b

entirely on that source? If we are not totally casting ourselves upon Him, but rather, making our own provision for ourselves, we cannot say that we have the Son, or that the Son has us.

Jesus said that if you could love those who spitefully use you, who curse you, who revile you, you will be the sons of your Father who is in heaven. He implies that the issue of sonship is the love of your enemies, and if we can do this, of what love, then, will we not be capable? These are they who have come into sonship, showing themselves to *be* the sons of the Father who is in heaven. This demonstration shows forth the Father. It is the very love that Jesus displayed at the cross, while we were yet enemies of God and in our sins.

Chapter 8

The Antiochal Pattern

Now there were at Antioch, in the church that was there, prophets and teachers: Barnabas, and Simeon who was called Niger, and Lucius of Cyrene, and Manaen who had been brought up with Herod the tetrarch, and Saul. While they were ministering to the Lord and fasting, the Holy Spirit said, "Set apart for Me Barnabas and Saul for the work to which I have called them." Then, when they had fasted and prayed and laid their hands on them, they sent them away. So, being sent out by the Holy Spirit, they went down to Seleucia and from there they sailed to Cyprus. When they reached Salamis, they began to proclaim the word of God in the synagogues of the Jews; and they also had John as their helper.[1]

---

[1] Acts 13:1-5

This episode sounds like a description of some idealistic phenomenon from the past, but having no relevance for today. However, I believe it is God's definitive pattern of missionary sending, from which we have grievously departed in this present hour. My spirit winces when I see my mail box stuffed with every kind of missionary and ministry appeal, all of the evidences of a melancholy abandonment of what has been offered us here as a true apostolic church and its mission activity.

The early churches were bodies of believers at a given geographical location. They were a besieged minority, saved out of the world, living in the midst of vicious hostility. They were standing gloriously by the power of the Spirit, who had full sway through their lives to the degree their fellowship together was authentically lived, face to face. No man thought that the things he owned were his own. They held all things common, and if any lacked, they sold their houses and properties and laid the proceeds at the feet of the apostles, who then made distribution to those in need.

Having established converts in the faith, Paul would take his leave, expecting to return a year or so later. The new believers remained and flourished in their localities because this one had a tongue, another had an interpretation, or a prophecy, or a revelation, or a teaching.[2] They had the full panoply of God as expressed through the brethren. They had God for a teacher with all the richness that the Spirit could provide in a true expression of the Body, and therefore, they had the assurance that God would not leave them comfortless. Each member was available to give an expression of the life of God every time they convened

---

[2] 1 Corinthians 14:26

together. Gatherings were a vital coming together of God's people for the edification of the assembly. The idea of passively sitting in pews, gazing at the back of the head of the person sitting in front of them while a salaried pastor conducted the service, was not the environment that they knew.

For many of us, the restoration of the apostolic pattern is going to be a very fearful adjustment, but there will not be any glorious works performed unless they are performed in this pattern, by the Holy Spirit, who shall separate men, by name, for the work whereunto *He* has called them. This is a lot different from the works we initiate, or involve ourselves in. The organizational mania of the world has captivated us more than we know. Anyone with a talent for administration, or knows how to hire those who have it, can quickly install himself in one kind of ministry or another; and so we have a Christendom that is congested with ministries and mission activities that never came from the will and purpose of God.

When the conditions for truth depart, the Holy Spirit goes also, and that is why we feel compelled to turn up the amplifiers, institute programs and add our own little innovations, thinking that by the increase of activity, we somehow have the reality. The same Holy Spirit, who put to death a man and a woman for presuming upon God by bringing only a part of the proceeds of a sale, is the same Holy Spirit still. There are many beautiful and glossy church buildings, and many programs, but we do not have the glory or the power of God, and we are therefore producing disciples who are fixated in a kind of self-centered infantilism.

When we depart from the apostolic pattern of God, especially in the light of what has been given to us in the Antiochal account, our teaching materials, messages, literature and conferences will be devoid of eternal fruit. Something of a lesser kind may be achieved, but the deeper issues of eternity will not be affected, and it is to those deeper issues that we are called.

"Now there were at Antioch, in the church that was there, prophets and teachers." They were *in* the church. This is very different from the casual aggregate of individualities that compose our present church situations. In the church at Antioch, they were deeply established; they were in a network of true spiritual relationship, one with another, which constitutes, in itself, the very nature of church. Compare that to our modern tendency to hop from one fellowship to another, wherever the grass might be greener, or the preaching more interesting, or the visiting speakers more winsome.

The structure and composition of the church at Antioch was conducive to the maturing of prophets, teachers and apostolic men. This is not the standard of measure that we employ today to test the health of our own fellowships. We would rather measure by numbers, or programs, or find some other kind of measure rather than ask ourselves whether we are a fellowship that is conducive to, and provides an environment for the nurturing and bringing forth of apostolic and prophetic men. If we are more zealous for the symmetry and order of our meetings than we are for the inconvenience and the pain of prophetic interruption, then we will never come to the God-desired pattern of the church at Antioch.

There are no two callings in God so dissimilar than teachers and prophets. In a certain sense, there is an antagonism and tension inherent in these callings toward each other. Authentic prophets and teachers are familiar with this tension. Teachers are systematic;

they see things as "line upon line and precept upon precept." Though a prophet insists on the scriptures as being the inspired statement of God, he often sees things intuitively. Being visionary, he sees the grander and larger picture. But a teacher recoils at the largesse and liberty that a prophet will take to himself. To the prophet, a teacher is narrow and limited, and yet, the episode begins by citing legitimate and valid callings, but callings that are, by their nature, intrinsically different to each other. The point is that these men have come through to something existentially, whereby their differences have not caused rupture or division, but rather, harmony, reconciliation and unity.

Unity in Diversity

Who were these prophets and teachers? Barnabas, a Jew; and Simeon that was called Niger, probably of African descent; and Lucius of Cyrene, one of the Mediterranean ethnic groups; and Manaen, who had been brought up with Herod the tetrarch, and possibly a Roman; and Saul, another Jew. What a conglomeration of backgrounds with every portent and possibility for conflict, strife and division. But they triumphed because "God was in Christ reconciling the world to Himself,"[3] and the essence of that reality had been established in their assembly.

Antioch is the pattern of apostolic reality and true sending. As far as we know, the church in Jerusalem that preceded it was uniquely Jewish, but the church in Antioch, with its ethnic, racial and cultural diversity, was found, *despite* those differences, "ministering to the Lord." This kind of unity can only be obtained through the deep workings of the cross in a people who

---

[3] See 2 Corinthians 5:19

are long enough and intensely enough together. They had come to a place of sanctification and separation from the things that make men resentful, irritated and jealous, and were therefore wholly given up to God *together*. We cannot minister to the Lord in truth when there are unspoken tensions and difficulties that have not been resolved between the brethren. We can sing songs and create a charismatic atmosphere through choruses, but is that worship to the Lord? Ministering to the Lord is an ultimate statement of a relationship to God in purity and priestly devotion that cannot be obtained independent of the brethren, but rather is obtained, as it were, *through* the brethren. There must be that relatedness to other believers, especially those who are different from us and who may be irritating to us *because* of those differences.

Priestly Ministration

It may well be that the first apostolic call came to men who were waiting on the Lord in priestly ministration in a silence more eloquent to God than the turned-up amplifiers of our contemporary worship services. It is one thing to be silent as an individual, but to be corporately silent in a room, face to face, is a form of suffering and death that few are willing to bear. Everything in us is itching for something to be said. Sound and sight are sensual things, and our senses constantly want to be gratified with something to hear, something to see, something to speak, something to do. Silence is therefore death to the senses, and asserts the primacy of the rule of God over our senses, which want to have an existence independent from Him. Thoughts that have their origin in man, even if they are ostensibly clean, and even of a religious or spiritual kind, are in God's sight unrighteous if they have not their origin in Him. Silence is the final death to anything that might yet linger in our self-sufficient, independent ability to serve God. Everything must be brought to death for true priestly ministration.

When God saw *that,* the Holy Spirit said, "Set apart for Me Barnabas and Saul for the work to which I have called them." In other words, they had reached something of an existential and authentic kind as was expressed in the authenticity of their worship together, thereby releasing the Lord to call and to send. God had something He could send to the world that would be a witness to the reality of a heavenly kingdom. Some transcendent breakthrough had occurred whereby the Holy Spirit could say, "I have found something that I want to replicate, a reality to which you have come. I can now send you because I have no fear that you are going to steal My glory. I *now* know that you are not going to go back home and send out newsletters to let everyone know of the great things I have done through you in Third World countries. I *now* know that you are not going to resort to carnal and soulish techniques and manipulations that disfigure and compromise religious activity, and which make it less than an apostolic, God-sanctioned work."

We all have unfathomed depths of carnality in our hearts, especially in the area of desiring opportunity for ministry. For those of us who were born poor or disadvantaged, there is fleshly tendency to want to prove to others that we now have a purpose in life. Who of us does not have an itch to want to be found acceptable and approved by others? For God to safely call us, an enormous depth of dealing is needed to bring us to a place of priestly rest and separation to Him. We are *all* riddled with defects and ambition; we *all* have blind spots. God's provision to attend to that, to perfect us and to bring us to a priestly and apostolic place, is *each other*. But if our fellowships are formal, structured in an institutional way, or have a pastoral master of ceremonies running the show, then we will not constitute a witness to our community, nor ever have true mission sending. If we are fostering a kind of pastoral mystique where the pastor is looked up to as somehow incapable of foibles and weaknesses, then we are promoting a deceptive unreality. Church leaders need to take those elevated platforms away, come down, and be exposed and seen as they truly are, as one among the brethren.

When Jesus said, "And you shall be witnesses unto Me," He did not mean that we were to do witnessing *for* Him. The *being* precedes the *doing*, and apostolic being precedes apostolic sending. Apostolic being is ultimate being and requires ultimate sacrifice to obtain. Of necessity, fervent love cannot have its full expression until we have broken through all the hurts, the disappointments and disillusionments we carry toward each other. Unfortunately, that is the very point where we run and seek another fellowship, or run off to another ministry. If we had only held steady at that point, and seen it through, and broke through to the transcendent ground of fervent love, then we would have heard the voice of the Spirit saying, "Set apart for Me..." Instead, our "sendings" are self-appointed missions, or responses to need, rather than the call of the Spirit, and therefore the consequences of our going are much less than the true works of God.

In Antioch, the believers were already a people set apart from their own racial differences, their strivings, their enmity, their suspicions, their resentments, their jealousies and their religious ambition. They would have been as content to remain in the place of worship as in the place of service. How many of us have come to the place where we no longer have any itch to go out and minister? We are just as content to remain in the place of anonymity, of being unseen, unknown and unheralded, as we are to be in the most conspicuous place of service. Only then can God send us, because He knows exactly when our one exclusive motive is the jealousy for His glory.

True Apostolic Work

We will not hear that call to send until we are a people who know how to fast and minister *unto the Lord*. Those men at Antioch did not go forth because they saw a great spiritual or social need. There is no more deadly snare for God's people than to elevate human need, or causes, or ministry calling above very God Himself. It is one of the most subtle of all deceptions and idolatries. They were called for the work whereunto *He* had called them, without expressly being told what that work was. They were not called to any specific ethnic group, or to any fulfillment of their gift or calling, but only *unto the Holy Spirit*, which is the only calling that is valid. In fact, if our work is directed toward a need, then we are not yet on apostolic ground. So much of what we do is birthed out of a sense of compulsion, a sense of religious obligation, a sense that we should be *doing* something for the needs that are everywhere around us. If those are our motivations, our works and actions will not redound to God's glory.

Though the scriptures say: "To the Jew first and also to the Greek,"[4] God did not send them expressly to the Jews, which would seem to be a contradiction.

---

[4] See Romans 1:16

But in being sent, and in the very unfolding of their sending by the Spirit, they ended up in Salamis preaching the word of God to the Jews in the synagogue. They did not take a scriptural principle and make of that their motivation for going. Being directed to the synagogue was a result of their union with the life of God. If we are incapable of waiting for the call of the Holy Spirit, then we are also incapable of serving. The apostolic work of God that shakes the earth, that has eternal consequence, is the kind that is initiated by the Holy Spirit, who calls men by name. Until we return to the pattern He has given us, we should not expect eternal results. We can do "good things," but we make void the eternal glory. Our ministry, if it is true ministry, should not be predicated upon where we know we are going, or what we are going to do, but simply *unto Him*. These were truly separated men, and that is why Paul could be turned away from the churches in Asia[5] that were being added to daily, and be brought to a place where the gospel had never been brought, namely, Macedonia, by a vision that came to him at night.

> When he had seen the vision, immediately
> we sought to go into Macedonia, concluding
> that God had called us to preach the gospel
> to them.[6]

Paul had the vision, but those who were traveling with him received *his* vision as God's call for *them*. There was no question as to whether the vision was legitimate. They recognized Paul's authority because they were in a quality of relationship with him that had been established, not on the road, but *in* the church at Antioch. The Spirit could turn them away from

---

[5] See Acts chapter 16
[6] Acts 16:10

successful evangelistic meetings because they were already a people set apart for Him. God is discreet, and does not lift the lid in order for us to see what happened in the formation of those men. Anyone who has lived seriously for God in an intensity of life with the brethren knows that it *must* have taken place. There is no shortcut to come to this place of unity, and would have necessarily been preceded by confrontations, struggles and tensions, and finally, reconciliation and resolution by the blood of the cross and the Spirit of God. There is no life without death, and these men had to taste that death. How long did Antioch exist before there was a sending? We are not told, but you can believe that there was a history of suffering before this glory.

The apostolic genius cannot be obtained independent of priestliness, and the heart of priestliness is the ability to wait upon God; it is the ability to minister unto Him in the place of devotion. Therefore, it is all the same whether one goes out to minister or remains. The going is worship, just as much as the remaining, but we all know, especially in the younger people, that there is an itch to go and to do for God. Our modern church life encourages us into that, and therefore we never come into the full maturation of the church, which is the matrix out of which true sending comes. What we have at Antioch is an apostolic matrix, a womb out of which something of a particular kind and quality is birthed and formed, which I believe God is yet waiting for in our own localities and nations.

Authority and Relationship

Recognizing authority does not come easily or automatically, and it is relative to our life and walk. The Thessalonian believers understood this, and that is why Paul could write to them:

> For this reason we also constantly thank God that when you received the word of God, which you heard from us, you accepted it not as the word of men, but for what it really is, the word of God, which also performs its work in you who believe.[7]

They knew it was God's word to them because Paul communicated a love and authority that was reflected in his words, compelling pagans to turn from their idols. Paul's authority came out of a life submitted to authority, especially to those with whom he was in relationship. Paul's apostolic call lay not only in what he intrinsically was in himself, but just as much in the character and stature of the fellowship that sent him.

> Then, when they [the congregation] had fasted and prayed and laid their hands on them, they sent them away. So, being sent out by the Holy Spirit...[8]

The laying on of the hands of that congregation *was* the sending forth of the Holy Spirit. This was the first apostolic journey, and Paul and Barnabas were not at all hesitant to allow those with whom they had been in fellowship in Antioch to lay hands on them and send them forth. The laying on of hands is a holy sacrament, and they had the assurance of knowing the

---

[7] 1 Thessalonians 2:13b
[8] Acts 13:3-4a

hands were of men whose character had been observed, tested and known. God equates the act of those men in sending forth Paul and Barnabas as being sent by the Holy Spirit. Not one of them had spent the previous evening flicking through the channels of their television set, or using their hands in any way that would have disqualified them. They were pure hands, and when you lay hands on someone, you transmit your condition *to* and *into* that person. The hands that were laid on Paul and Barnabbas were of the same character and substance as their own. The laying on of hands is one of the most profound covenantal acts that men can perform with each other in God's sight. It is a commitment of a kind that makes that very sending possible. It implicates the one whose hands were used in the sending to be as deeply involved in the character of the work as the one who goes.

They were a fellowship who understood these things, and recognized how significant and fateful Paul and Barnabas' speaking and conduct were to be. In the laying on of hands, they were saying, "We not only identify with you, we sustain you by our intercessions; we are going to suffer the consequence of what you are doing; we are one with you in this." They were now under obligation to sustain the sent ones by their prayers. Any intercession for the men who had been sent that was not out of this quality of relationship would be a mere performance. It would only have been a religious obligation, a sense of requirement that does not impress God. True intercession and true prayer are forms of dying. We can all pray, but the kind of prayer that is an agony of groanings that cannot be uttered is a form of dying. Sadly, we are far removed from realities of this kind, and so much the reflection of a superficial world that is satisfied with only nominal things and verbal understandings, being more content with a *ceremonial* laying on of hands that is much less and other than the true thing.

In any true sending, there can be no assurance that those being sent are ever going to return. It is a painful, heart-breaking moment because you have opened yourself for love and made yourself vulnerable. You have gone beyond a "full-gospel bear hug," and come into a place where that brother has become so dear, that if he does not come back, it will be a loss that you cannot even begin to calculate. Are we willing to go that far in God, or do we want to safeguard ourselves from the pain of that kind of intensive love and affection for the brethren? If we are individualistically-minded and centered in our own personal ministries, then we will not realize to what degree true ministry comes out of the life, and the life out of the relationships. True ministry is never out of one man's virtuoso ability or singular calling. The content of his message and the character of his life need first to be wrought into him in the context of true fellowship.

Paul and Barnabas' setting apart took place *before* they were sent, *in* the church; it was there that they were sifted, purified and purged in the sanctifying process of God, in and through the Body of Christ, where the brethren "speak the truth in love" in all of the time and patience and sacrifice that such speaking requires. There is nothing more needful in this hour than men and women who are willing again for that sacrifice, willing to leave places of comfort and familiarity in order to come into that matrix of fellowship and relationship. Are we willing to forsake our present privatistic mode of living in order to obtain a future Antioch?

Filling up the Suffering

The scriptures speak about the sufferings that remain to be filled up in Christ. To be in a conventional church situation, and to be struggling in it, or to be rejected in it, and to have to sit through it, Sunday after Sunday, without any seeming hope, in all of the sense of despair and alienation, is a suffering that *must* be borne. We are not called to reject those places or to flee from them, but to remain faithful *in* them and to guard ourselves as to how we speak and relate to them. It must not be in any critical way, but usually bearing it in silence unless the Lord gives us the liberty to speak. We need to look to the Lord to bring the influences that will move it from where it presently is to what it needs to become. The end of the age is upon us; there are centrifugal forces working to move us either radically toward or away from God, and it will make it necessary for those churches to decide whether they will go, likewise, toward or away from God.

This is an hour of preparation for soon-coming realities for which many of us are not prepared. It is an hour of restoration for a flabby and anemic church that has played too long with its charismatic toys and evangelical dryness. It is a church that needs to be restored to apostolic reality in the spirit of truth. We cannot call to repentance a world that is dying and facing the judgments of God until there is a kingdom of God which is at hand *amongst us*. We need to come again to be the apostolic people of God, showing forth the kingdom, that men might repent and be saved.

Chapter 9

The Preached Word

Preaching the word of God is much more than a word
of biblical orientation; it is more than the correct
formulation of the doctrines of God. The word of God
is a divine communication of a uniquely powerful kind
that God intends to be expressed through a human
vessel.   Paul's   own   acute   awareness   of   the
phenomenon is expressed in his first epistle to the
Thessalonians:

> For this reason we also constantly thank
> God that when you received the word of
> God which you heard from us, you accepted
> it not as the word of men, but for what it
> really is, the word of God, which also
> performs its work in you who believe.[1]

We need to read this as a literal and accurate
description of a particular mode of speaking rare in our
own   time.   If   the   distinctive   nature   of   this

---

[1] 1 Thessalonians 2:13

communication is its power, what then is its character? Paul is careful to instruct his Greek correspondents, contrary to their own culture and love of rhetoric, that the preaching of the gospel can actually be voided of its power if it is expressed in the eloquent wisdom of men. The word of God is qualitatively different from human eloquence, and if we lapse into that, we void the statement of its power.

We need a deep and new appreciation for the holy sacrament of preaching because believers, and particularly ministers, are forever seeking to establish their reputations and their acceptance on some basis other than the preached word.

The first statement of the anointed ministry of Jesus took place in a synagogue, in the reading of a portion of Isaiah 61: "The Spirit of the Lord is upon Me because He anointed Me to preach..."[2] There is a conjunction between anointing and true preaching. The preached word has a particular quality that distinguishes it from any other kind of speaking or oratory. Preaching is a remarkable phenomenon, even a matter of life and death because:

> How then will they call on Him in whom they have not believed? How will they believe in Him whom they have not heard? And how will they hear without a preacher? How will they preach unless they are sent?[3]

The preaching of one who is sent is at the heart of the whole mission and calling of the church to the unbelieving world. He whom *God* sends is given the Spirit without measure. This sending is therefore critical for which reason God establishes local bodies

---

[2] See Luke 4:18
[3] Romans 10:14-15a

of believers, because we have to be sent from somewhere.

The Word of the Cross

> For the word of the cross is foolishness to those who are perishing, but to us who are being saved it is the power of God.[4]
>
> For since in the wisdom of God the world through its wisdom did not come to know God, God was well-pleased through the foolishness of the message preached to save those who believe.[5]

The word of the cross *is* the power of God; it contains an inherent, divinely penetrating ability to register divine truths *despite* the severest religious, cultural and ethnic resistance, as well as an ability to create faith in the hearer, causing him to believe unto salvation. It is the word of God as "event," and an event not necessarily under auspicious circumstances. It performs a work in them that believe, or a work that has brought them to the place of believing. It is a heavenly word proclaimed in the earth, not only to those who may be willing hearers, but also, and just as much, to those who are resistant hearers. Earth resists heaven, and every power of darkness wants to cloud the minds of men and keep them from understanding and responding. Therefore, a word of an ultimate kind is needed like a hammer on a rock to break that resistance.

The word of the cross is not necessarily the statement or description of the actual crucifixion of

---

[4] 1 Corinthians 1:18
[5] Ibid., v.21

Jesus. There is another meaning implicit in this phrase, even when the cross itself is not necessarily the subject matter. The substance of the crucifixion event, replicated in the humiliation of the preaching, is the re-enactment of the cross-experience itself. Every time the cross is re-enacted in any humiliation that comes from an obedience, the power that was demonstrated at the cross is again given opportunity to be expressed, proportionate to the degree to what is actually borne or suffered in that humiliation.

The reason we see so little of the power of God in preaching is that men take pains to avoid the humiliation of the cross, preferring to play it safe with man-deferring sermons. There is an unwillingness to take the risk of failure and to trust God for the word *in that moment*. There is a genuine place for sermon preparation, but in the preaching event itself, room must be made for God, and if we insulate ourselves from God by our own religious, human and professional preparation, we void the operation of the cross and the foolishness of it, namely, the suffering and the humiliation, and therefore the power of the cross. No matter what a man's natural qualifications and strengths, he must, in that tremulous moment, be in weakness and much trembling.

A preacher, who intentionally empties himself in trust for the word of God to be given, will, in the dying to his own ability to speak, experience a measure of suffering akin to that of the crucified Christ. He becomes foolish in a humiliation unto death like the Savior's before him. This is the heart of all true speaking. The man speaking sees to it that his own ability will not be his dependency or source of supply. God does not want the faith of men to be established on human eloquence, but only on the basis of the power of God.

In much preaching and ministry, we more often than not lean on our own human ability. I think that is basically a description of what goes on in the majority of Sunday morning services. There is something in the scriptures themselves that has a vivifying effect, or the people would be without profit altogether. But the preaching that is the power of God comes when a man abandons himself, and will not lean on his own expertise, his own savvy or his own ability. Pulling out *that* plug is the death. It is something one can never get used to, but is to be tasted again and again. Every occasion is as terrifying and mortifying as if you had never done it before. It is a recurring experience in death. Who is willing to taste those kinds of death? Who is willing to abandon his own proven and trusted ability and confidence, and trust that the same power that raised Jesus from the dead will now raise the speaker and his message?

The Creative Word

The Lord's obedient suffering unto death, by which the veil of the Temple was rent, is again re-enacted by the preacher's obedience, but this time, the veil is rent over the heart and darkened mind of the hearer. This not only emits light on what is otherwise patently foolish and offensive to human sensibility, but it births or creates the grace of repentance and faith unto believing.

A correctly recited word out of the Bible is not necessarily *the* word of God. It is only the word of God when it is the word *given*, and that word does not necessarily have to be a written canonical word to be a word of God. It is not a word that will contradict the scriptures, but it could be a word of mocking, or insult, or confrontation, or a strange and foolish word. Those who speak the words of God have already come to a sufficient death to themselves that the power of God can be measured out to them without any danger that the glory of God will be touched or misappropriated.

Given the absence of the deep conversions effected by the preaching of the word in our own generation, one wonders if we have sufficiently considered the meaning of the word "sent." Have we naïvely assumed that *any* promulgation of the gospel is blessed and honored of God? If preaching Christ is more than the message *about* Him, but rather the showing forth *of* Him, then the God who sends may yet be waiting for suitable candidates for His sending. The issue is the issue of the cross, and one might rightly suspect that the word of God will not come to men with full conviction, except through the lips of those who know the cross in their own experience, and are willing to suffer the humiliation of it again and again in the very foolishness of their speaking. If our speaking is not foolishness, then it is not a true speaking. It may amuse men, it may even inform them, but it will *never* be an event.

To preach truly is not the issue of skill or learned technique, but a divine mystery. The very word "preaching" is derived from the Latin word *praedikare*, which means "to make known." Whenever Christ's humiliation is explicated in the foolishness of preaching, He is again revealed and set forth to be the Savior. For just as God gives grace to the humble, so also does He, who is full of grace and truth, have opportunity to intersect time and eternity, heaven and earth, in the moment of authentic meekness when a preacher ceases from himself.

A familiar illustration of this cruciform life is to be found in Paul's first letter to the Corinthians where he writes:

> And when I came to you, brethren, I did not come with superiority of speech or of wisdom, proclaiming to you the testimony of God. For I determined to know nothing among you except Jesus Christ, and Him crucified.[6]

For all of Paul's erudition and religious knowledge, this kind of self-imposed limitation required a painful determination. The trouble is that we know so much, and so much that we know wants to find expression. Therefore, it requires a determination to put away what is so accessible and available to our preaching.

God will not give His glory to another, except when it is exclusively *Himself* being expressed by the preacher, and that is why we do not see *that* glory, because not many of us are willing to live on that razor's edge. We are not so much concerned with the glory of God as avoiding the embarrassment of failure. That is why we have so little resurrection event in our weekly pulpit preaching. That is why true preaching is different from conventional preaching, which can never be an event in God. As someone has said, and I believe it out of my own experience: "Every true preaching is a raising again of the dead." We need to have an enhanced appreciation for what resurrection means as a "God-event" in the word that is spoken in resurrection power. We will never be a mouthpiece for God if we are trying to preserve our reputation, or if we are afraid ourselves to experience death, and that is why we do not see the glory of God.

---

[6] 1 Corinthians 2:1-2

The man who loves to talk, loves to be public, who enjoys being seen and heard, will never speak the word of event. The man who sighs and groans when he gets up to the pulpit, and would rather that the floor open up and swallow him, who does not want to be there, who feels terribly uncomfortable, and who knows that he is not going to be understood, is the man out of whose mouth the word of true preaching is most likely to come. Like Jonah, who wanted to escape the call of God, the man who does not want to preach is the only one qualified to preach.

In an hour in which biblical faith is eroding, many of us are content with mere scriptural or doctrinal correctness. How urgent it is, then, to elevate the church's whole level of regard and expectation for the word to be a creative event, producing change and establishing faith in the hearer; a word beyond that which is merely informational. In my observation, we do not have this expectation. We do not come together to hear the word *of God,* but rather a word *about* God, by a man himself who does not believe that he is speaking the word *of God.* It is the *word* that is the event, not the stylistic presentation, and when we attempt to bring a stylistic presentation, we rob the word of its power and we lapse into human eloquence.

Where that creative word is not expressed, the sermon stands in jeopardy of becoming mere ceremony, a piece of familiar and unchallenging predictability. It requires nothing from its hearers and it makes no demand; it only fills the space that has been made for it, and there is no glory in the church; we have only been sermonized. To be sermonized week after week will have a dulling affect on our spirits and discernment. To that measure, we are incapacitated as God's agents in the world, and constitute only a sleepy Sunday religious culture that the world can well afford to ignore. The faith is holy. We cannot live, transact and operate our lives as though this were not so, and think that there will be no consequence of any kind.

How out of tune our contemporary preaching is to the whole tenor of Paul's exhortation to Timothy: "Preach the word; be ready in season and out of season; reprove, rebuke, exhort, with great patience and instruction."[7] Evidently, to preach the word was to be particular, pointed and uncompromising in confronting the brethren on the condition of their lives and the necessity for change; and they knew it.

In our age of ministerial professionalism, degree credentials from institutions of learning carry more weight than being authentically and apostolically charged for the call of ministry. This is only a symptom of the yet larger problem, namely, the substitution of the glory of God in the church for a man-pleasing *ethos*. That is why we have such shallow teaching and preaching. God is not giving His authority and depth to men who would use and usurp it for their own ends, their own names and their religious success.

True Preaching Waits on True Sending

Everything rests on the preacher being *sent*. This means that the fellowship sending him is of one mind with him. They necessarily share the same mentality and cross-centeredness, or God would not say, "Set apart for Me." To be sent is much more than being commissioned; it is to be sent in place of another. The

---

[7] 2 Timothy 4:2

Other is Christ Himself, and it is through those who are sent that the people hear Christ's voice and speech:

> But what does it say? "THE WORD IS NEAR YOU, IN YOUR MOUTH AND IN YOUR HEART," that is, the word of faith which we are preaching, that if you confess with your mouth Jesus as Lord and believe in your heart that God raised Him from the dead, you will be saved; for with the heart a person believes, resulting in righteousness, and with the mouth he confesses, resulting in salvation. For the Scripture says, "WHOEVER BELIEVES IN HIM WILL NOT BE DISAPPOINTED." For there is no distinction between Jew and Greek; for the same Lord is Lord of all, abounding in riches for all who call upon Him; for "WHOEVER WILL CALL ON THE NAME OF THE LORD WILL BE SAVED." How then will they call on Him in whom they have not believed? How will they believe in Him whom they have not heard? And how will they hear without a preacher? How will they preach unless they are sent? Just as it is written, "HOW BEAUTIFUL ARE THE FEET OF THOSE WHO BRING GOOD NEWS OF GOOD THINGS!" However, they did not all heed the good news; for Isaiah says, "LORD, WHO HAS BELIEVED OUR REPORT? So faith comes from hearing, and hearing by the word of Christ."[8]

Much of modern day evangelism has reduced the gospel to a formula, putting before the hearer an "easy-

---

[8] Romans 10:8-17

believism," which has left many outside the kingdom. The hearers recite a repeat-after-me prayer, thus missing the whole profound point. There is a certain kind of hearing that is required for a certain kind of believing, and to emphasize this, Paul quotes from the Book of Isaiah where the prophet says:

> How lovely on the mountains are the feet of him who brings good news, who announces peace and brings good news of happiness, who announces salvation, and says to Zion, "Your God reigns!"[9]

This verse is preceded by something remarkable in verse 6:

> Therefore My people shall know My name; therefore in that day I am the one who is speaking, "Here I am."

The word "announce" is better understood as meaning "pronounce" or "proclaim." It is more than an announcement of information; it is a word that constitutes an event when it is sounded. It is a creative word of God, a *rhema* word, in the hearing of which an event occurs, and faith is established where there was none before.

To propound the faith to others in a systematic way by which their logic can be satisfied, so that they can be won over by some kind of invincible logic of statements, is not the basis by which God desires to reveal Himself. He says that the key to their believing, and their calling on the name of the Lord, is the hearing of a particular word, namely, the *word of Christ Himself.* The feet of those who bear good news are called lovely, or blessed, because God is the One who is speaking, "Here I am." God is the One who possesses that earthen vessel, and therefore it is

---

[9] Isaiah 52:7

113

actually Christ's *own* word. They hear the voice of God, and His word is as creative as it was in the beginning when He spoke and it came into being.

In other words, the voice, the speaking, the content and the words that constitute the creative event that establishes faith to believe, enabling the hostile and resistant to call on God's name, is actually His voice and His speaking. We might believe it could come through some giants of the faith like Paul, but can we believe for the phenomenon to come through ourselves? Or that God could have the full possession of us, who are the sons and daughters of resurrection, that we might say with absolute certitude, "It is He who is speaking, here He is!"?

Unless those being addressed hear Christ's message and voice, they will not believe the truths of His death and resurrection. If you believe in your heart that Jesus is Lord, and that God has raised Him from the dead, you shall be saved, but how shall they believe on Him unless they believe that He was raised from the dead? And how shall they believe that He was raised from the dead except that the evidence of the resurrection is in the words, the demeanor, the voice and the disposition of the man who stands before them? How can they believe unless they see the truth of the resurrection in those who bring the word? Nothing less will bring about the salvation of the unsaved, and particularly the unsaved Jew in the last days.

Resurrection Life

The issue of the resurrection is inextricably linked to the authenticity of the lordship of Jesus in the believer's life.

Being found in appearance as a man, He humbled Himself by becoming obedient to the point of death, even death on a cross. For this reason also, God highly exalted Him, and bestowed on Him the name which is above every name, so that at the name of Jesus EVERY KNEE WILL BOW, of those who are in heaven and on earth and under the earth, and that every tongue will confess that Jesus Christ is Lord, to the glory of God the Father.[10]

The resurrection of Jesus is the exaltation of the One who experienced an ultimate humiliation unto death. His lordship consists of His being exalted above every name, and that is what is conferred upon Him through His resurrection for His obedience unto death. That is why "whosoever confesses that Jesus is Lord and believes in their heart that God has raised Him from the dead shall be saved."[11] Lordship and resurrection are inextricably joined together.

In seeing the evidence of the resurrection of Christ in the messenger and hearing the voice of the resurrected Christ, the unbeliever, who has had no preparation for this encounter, is faced with the end of the lordship over *his* own life; he will no longer determine what he is going to do. When Jesus becomes Lord, our self-will and self-determination end, and God says, "Now you'll do *My* bidding." The reason why people are offended at God, who would otherwise enjoy God as God, is because they do not like the *Lord* part; it is the lordship that catches us in the throat, because none of us likes to be told what to do. Believing unto salvation is more than giving God a

---

[10] Philippians 2:8-11
[11] See Romans 10:9-10

little honorific acknowledgment; it means the once-and-for-all surrender of an independent life to the totality of God's authority.

The messenger must himself be a son or daughter of the resurrection, or he would not be a true witness. The fellowship out of which he comes must be a fellowship of a resurrected people, who live in the power and the reality of resurrection, or there is no true sending. The whole issue is the truth of resurrection as it is experientially known by a people in the earth, or both Jew and Gentile remain bound in their unbelief and self-will.

The one who is bringing the good news of a God who reigns is the same one in whom God reigns *in fact*. Though those who are hearing him cannot articulate what they are sensing, the truth of His reigning as Lord is demonstrated in the posture, the voice, the face, the demeanor and the character of the one who brings the glad tidings.

In the last analysis, the world is dying for the lack of the communication of very God Himself, and it is this reality that is the apostolic message and the foundation of the church.

Chapter 10

Prayer and Worship

We had prayer meetings virtually every day in our community fellowship, and there were occasions when those meetings were agonizing and painful. We sat in silence, looking at each other face to face. Nobody had a prayer, nobody had a word, nobody had a thought, and we waited and we waited and we waited. Silence is death to the senses, and asserts the primacy of the rule of God over those things which want to have an independent existence from Him. Waiting is a form of dying, and we could have alleviated that uneasiness. We were clever enough; we could have said something, we could have broken into a chorus. This denial of self was a redemptive suffering for the purposes of God until, finally, someone prayed something, or shared something, and the sessions that began in that kind of painful death frequently ended in glory.

Authentic prayer and authentic praise and worship are themselves a re-enactment of the cross by our

117

willingness to forsake and put aside human confidence and dependence, and come trembling and dependent upon God, willing to experience the foolishness of weakness. Are our prayers of the safe and timid kind? Are our prayers conventional and respectable? Are they *our* prayers conceived in *our* own minds? Or are they God's prayers? Have we ever let go of the one in order to obtain the other? It is a fearful proposition to die to our own prayers, because we will never know what form our prayer will then take, or what its content will be. And even if we begin a prayer, will we be able to end it? And how will it sound? Will it embarrass us? Will it confuse those who hear it? There are many forms of suffering unto humiliation and death, and the truth of the cross for the church is the *daily* dying. Failure, humiliation and what men might think will keep us fearful. We are afraid to take the risks of faith, lest we fail. Failure is death; humiliation is death, but in the kingdom of God, it is *the way* of life.

The quality and authenticity of our corporate prayer cannot exceed the quality and authenticity of our relationships in our life together. In other words, true prayer is relative to the quality and truth of the corporate life *together*. Prayer is not the issue of virtuosity or skill; it is the statement of the truth of the corporate life. Are we in a place of union and identification with the Lord *together*, or are we disjointed and isolated individual entities, who have not a significant and authentic reality in relationship among ourselves? The cross has both a horizontal and vertical beam; they both must be authentically joined. We delude ourselves to think that we can have a vertical relationship with God, and yet be forgetful of our neighbor. The safest way to measure our spirituality and relationship to God is not by our euphoric visions of the heavenlies, but by the truth of our relationship with that flesh-and-blood neighbor right next to us!

There is a place for private, personal prayer, but not in a corporate setting. True corporate prayer is the issue of the corporate life, and it is only this kind of prayer that does business with the principalities and the powers of the air over our communities and nations. The powers of darkness are required to acknowledge only what is authentic in us.

The assembling of the brethren is much more than coming together for a meeting; it is an existential participation by each member in the drama and dynamic of the full life of the fellowship. "When you come together, each one has...," but where does the first person begin? Our tendency today is to have a salaried minister or talented worship leader to act as a master of ceremonies, and who inevitably pre-determines *which* songs will be sung and *when* they will be sung. The format of the service follows a proven and acceptable pattern. In my opinion, the use of overhead projectors, plasma screens, elaborate music teams, hi-tech amplifiers and mixers, and other techniques designed to prod the people into worship are contrary to the freedom of the Holy Spirit.

True praise and worship ought to be the spontaneous overflow of joy and praise to God for the depth and truth of His sanctifying work in us. In other words, true praise is an unpremeditated and unorchestrated expression of gratitude for a reality that has come corporately through redemptive suffering in people who are together long enough and intensely enough to obtain it. When the powers of the air hear *that*, they are required to flee. Our worship will never exceed the quality of our relationships. We can turn up the amplifiers all we want, we can create a euphoric musical atmosphere, and yet still be deceived.

Worship is more than singing. The heart of worship is sacrifice, and there is nothing more sacrificial than the loss of our privacy and our individualism when we give ourselves in earnest relationship one to another. The high Christian divorce rate, the immorality, the divisions and splits, the hopping from one fellowship to another, and everything else that splits a fellowship asunder are testimony to our preferring a lesser, humanly-contrived alternative to the organic work of God in our corporate life.

Chapter 11

Confession: The Breakthrough to True Fellowship

There is hardly another writer who has understood the subject of confession of sin, or who has expressed it so incisively as Dietrich Bonhoeffer. In Nazi Germany prior to World War II, and in the intensity of community life, things came to the surface that he would not have otherwise seen, and in the midst of that, Bonhoeffer caught a glimpse of the reality of what enables church to be the expression of the Lord's life.

He begins the final chapter of his book, *Life Together*[1], with the Scripture: "Confess your sins to one another."[2] Like so many of God's scriptural prescriptions, we simply do not do them, and therefore suffer the loss of what God has given us as a precious

---

[1] *Life Together* by Dietrich Bonhoeffer, published by Harper and Row. Copyright, 1954. Used with permission
[2] See James 5:16

provision to be freed from a weight we need not bear. Every true act of obedience is a humiliation; it is another ascent to the cross, but it always eventuates in another resurrection *unto life*. To confess our faults one to another is prickly, shameful and embarrassing. By nature, we prefer to confess privately and personally in our own closets, and hope that this will accomplish the same thing, and that by so doing, we believe we have actually *done* the word of God. But Bonhoeffer writes:

> He who is alone with his sin is utterly alone...It may be that Christians, notwithstanding corporate worship, common prayer, and all their fellowship in service, may still be left to their loneliness.[3]

To be separated from the brethren, leading an isolated life, is not a statement of our temperament; it is a statement of our sin. We may not have recognized it as that, because the first propensity of sin is to conceal itself as sin; and how many of us have become adept at finding ways of excusing ourselves from the assembling of the brethren? And even when we may be *positionally* present, for all intents and purposes, we are not *actually* there. Sin will break fellowship, and unconfessed sin condemns us to being apart from the Body, and therefore not receiving the benefit *of* the Body.

> The final breakthrough to fellowship does not occur, because, though they have fellowship with one another as believers and as devout people, they do not have fellowship as the undevout, as sinners.[4]

---

[3] *Life Together* by Dietrich Bonhoeffer, page 110
[4] Ibid., page 110

In other words, except that we have fellowship as sinners, we do not have fellowship. As sinners, we can take the mask off and put the pretense and sham away, and present ourselves to a brother as we in fact are before God. This is the foundation for true fellowship. Wearing our best religious faces is not true fellowship. True fellowship comes from the brethren who acknowledge that they are sinners being saved by grace. But it must be a very real and trembling truth for those who know that their iniquity is ever before them. The fellowship needs to be aware of its own defects, shortcomings and sin, so that it can admit the presence of another as a sinner. The sinner must not feel he needs to withdraw himself in the consciousness of his own sin. There needs to be an environment whereby he can confess his sins to another, that he might be prayed for and be healed. Confessing one's sin to another is speaking the truth in love, even when it is the truth about oneself.

> The pious [or "religious"] fellowship permits no one to be a sinner. We dare not be sinners. Many Christians are unthinkably horrified when a real sinner is suddenly discovered among the righteous. So we remain alone with our sin, living in lies and hypocrisy. The fact is that we are sinners![5]
>
> But it is the grace of the Gospel, which is so hard for the pious to understand, that it confronts us with the truth and says: You are a sinner, a great, desperate sinner; now come, as the sinner that you are, to God who loves you. He wants you as you are; He does not want anything from you, a sacrifice, a work; He wants you alone...God

---

[5] Ibid., page 110

has come to you to save the sinner. Be glad!
This message is liberation through truth.[6]

God will meet us on the basis of truth, when all phoniness and pretense has been put away. He Himself is truth, and His grace is freely and copiously available. So many Christian lives remain fixed at an unhappy level because they do not meet God on the level of truth, and the evidence of that is that they do not meet the brethren on the level of truth. We can measure the truth of our relationship with God by our relationship with men. If it is deceitful, phony, secretive, withholding and unloving there, then our relationship with God is no better. The two are inextricably joined. It is our relationship *to* men that unmasks us, and it is our relationship *with* men that is the true requirement.

Sinners Saved by Grace

> The mask you wear before men will do you no good before Him [God]…He wants to be gracious to you. You do not have to go on lying to yourself and your brothers, as if you were without sin; you can dare to be a sinner...The misery of the sinner and the mercy of God: this was the truth of the Gospel in Jesus Christ. It was in this truth that His church was to live.[7]

True fellowship begins with the most foundational recognition of ourselves as sinners being saved by grace. This grace is ministered one to another in the environment of *truth in love*, where one *can* confess

---

[6] Ibid., page 110-111
[7] Ibid., page 111

one's faults. To secretly hold our faults and sins is to block fellowship and the flow of the life of God into and through the whole Body. Speaking the truth in love cannot easily take place in a large institutional setting in which you can wear a religious and devout face, while all the time fighting secret and private battles. Those sitting near you have no knowledge of your struggles, and then, when the plastic communion cups are passed around, you take your cup, and they take theirs, but the whole thing is a sham.

To continue in that unreality will void and nullify the very provision that God intended to be our life, our vitality and our growth, because we have not understood that there cannot be communion without there first being confession. Confession frees us to take the cup; it frees us from condemning ourselves to judgment, to sickness and to physical and spiritual death. The very thing that God intends for life will be death if we take it while *not discerning the Body*.[8] If we are unwilling to see the things that need to be attended to, and be brought into the light and be submitted to the blood of Christ, that we might have true fellowship one with another, then we make communion a sham.

> Our brother has become Christ for us in the power and authority of the commission Christ has given to him. Our brother stands before us as the sign of the truth and the grace of God. He has been given to us to help us. He hears the confession of our sins in Christ's stead and he forgives our sins in Christ's name. He keeps the secret of our

---

[8] See 1 Corinthians 11:27-32

> confession as God keeps it. When I go to
> my brother to confess, I am going to God.[9]

Confessing our faults one to another, and praying for one another, that we might be healed, keeps fellowship clean, flowing and true.

> So in the Christian community when the call
> to brotherly confession and forgiveness goes
> forth, it is a call to the great grace of God in
> the church.[10]

It is a great grace to be free from sin and to have the weight and the guilt of it broken and dismissed. We need not shamefully withhold ourselves for fear of being detected. We can come open-faced and be in relationship with the brethren with nothing to fear and nothing to withhold. The substitute for that is a pious taking of our confession to God privately. It is giving to God a subterfuge and deception because we are unwilling for the shame, which is to say, the cross-experience of going to a brother.

Conventional church, as it is presently constituted, does not provide an environment for confessing of faults one to another. We do not know each other well enough to trust each other sufficiently for such an intimate thing as the confession of our faults. Therefore, we end up keeping our sins to ourselves, maintaining the façade of religious piety, when inwardly we are contradicted; and we know it because our words do not have the ringing sound of full conviction.

It is the issue of sin and compromise at the foundation of the inward life that has not been brought to the light because we are not in a church situation that is conducive to confession and deliverance. The

---

[9] *Life Together* by Dietrich Bonhoeffer, pages 111-112
[10] Ibid., page 112

whole fellowship then becomes a façade, and the members play-act the faith. And if that is happening at the deepest levels of the church, namely, its leadership and its ministry, what then is happening among the people who are under this leadership? Something happens in the whole atmosphere of the fellowship by which the same kind of duplicity, hiding and deceit take place, going on week after week in a kind of charade while the world is dying everywhere around it.

"In confession the breakthrough to community takes place."[11] We may enjoy singing choruses and hearing inspiring speakers, but true fellowship has, at its heart, the truth of the confessing of faults one to another. See to this and the choruses will take care of themselves. Through musical instruments, amplifiers and human ability, it is easy to create a euphoric aura of enjoyment in worship, but which, in reality, disguises rather than reflects what the true state of that fellowship is. We will deceive ourselves into thinking that we have a quality of relationship with God that in all actuality *does not exist*, because we do not have it with each other.

"In the darkness of the unexpressed it [unconfessed sin] poisons the whole being of a person."[12] Unconfessed sin will work its cancerous work when we keep it private and to ourselves. In our pride, we would rather die and suffer a spiritual death than a death to our ego. Without humility it is impossible to receive anything from God, and here is a perfect case in point. Here is health waiting, here is grace waiting, here is mercy and deliverance waiting, but pride keeps one from receiving it.

---

[11] Ibid., page 112
[12] Ibid., page 112

> In confession the light of the Gospel breaks into the darkness and seclusion of the heart. The sin must be brought into the light. The unexpressed must be openly spoken and acknowledged. It is a hard struggle until the sin is openly admitted.[13]

God has intended that the place of healing is in the fellowship, not only for the sheep, but also for the shepherds. Our shepherds are in as much need of healing and deliverance as the sheep; there is no magic about their lives. They are flesh and blood like as we. They may be anointed in the operation of their gift and calling, but in terms of their character and life, their needs and defects are equally as great as our own. Are they in an environment where their defects can be expressed?

> Since the confession of sin is made in the presence of a Christian brother, the last stronghold of self-justification is abandoned. The sinner surrenders; he gives up all his evil. He gives his heart to God.[14]

The last stronghold of man is self-justification. Whenever we are confronted, we always seem to marshal our excuses and have our reasons to justify and defend ourselves. When that is abandoned and the sinner surrenders, the breakthrough comes.

Daily Vigilance

> He finds the forgiveness of all his sin in the fellowship of Jesus Christ and his brother. The expressed, acknowledged sin has lost

---

[13] Ibid., page 112
[14] Ibid., page 112

all its power. It has been revealed and judged as sin. It can no longer tear the fellowship asunder. Now the fellowship bears the sin of the brother. He is no longer alone with his evil for he has cast off his sin in confession and handed it over to God. It has been taken away from him. Now he stands in the fellowship of sinners who live by the grace of God in the cross of Jesus Christ.[15]

When the breakthrough to true fellowship has occurred, we need to maintain that reality. If we are lazy, slothful, fearful and casual, and unwilling to pay the price of speaking the truth in love, taking a brother aside, or receiving a word of correction when it comes, sickness will again come into the fellowship. We need to keep our corporate heart with all vigilance, being jealous over it, because its Head is the Lord, and He will not do anything except through His Body.

Now he can be a sinner and still enjoy the grace of God. He can confess his sins and in this very act find fellowship for the first time. The sin concealed separated him from the fellowship, made all his apparent fellowship a sham. The sin confessed has helped him to find true fellowship with the brethren in Jesus Christ.

A confession of sin in the presence of all the members of the congregation is not required to restore one to fellowship with the whole congregation. I meet the whole congregation in the one brother to whom I confess my sins and who forgives my sins. In the fellowship I find with this one

---

[15] Ibid., pages 112-113

129

> brother, I have already found fellowship
> with the whole congregation. In confession
> occurs the breakthrough to the Cross.
>
> Confession in the presence of a brother is
> the profoundest kind of humiliation. It
> hurts, it cuts a man down, it is a dreadful
> blow to pride. To stand there before a
> brother as a sinner is an ignominy that is
> almost unbearable. In the confession of
> concrete sins the old man dies a painful,
> shameful death in the eyes of a brother.[16]

Even in confession we can side-step the reality of
the cross. We can make a play at it, talk around it,
make an allusion to it, and still come out with our pride
intact. God intends that pride be crucified in the very
act of confession, in proportion to the specificity of it.
Our natural propensity is to rationalize our sin and to
avoid being specific about it, but the cross *only*
becomes the cross in the specificity and the
concreteness of the sin acknowledged. That is where it
hurts and the shame is ignited. That is where the truth
of it is registered.

The *real* death comes in the painful, humiliating
confession of the fault to another. That very
humiliation *is* the death; it is the experiential
application of the death to a sin that would otherwise
continue its life. Our pride remains intact when we
make our own private confessions to God. That
stubborn and carnal thing, which still has a powerful
existence, will not go away, and the only thing that
brings it to an actual death *in fact* is the humiliation of
confession to another. In so doing, one tastes the death
of humiliation, which the Lord Himself tasted in much
greater measure when He was crucified publicly and

---

[16] Ibid., page 113

nakedly. He, who was made sin, bore that openly, shamefully and totally. How then can we allow ourselves the luxury of privacy? Taking up the cross means sharing in the shame of exposure through open confession and the revealing of our sin. Self will not be brought to death until we suffer it in the measure that the Lord did, that is to say, publicly and openly. If we do not burn in that humiliation, then we have probably not been truthful. We are still saving and protecting something, and therefore, we are cheating both ourselves and the fellowship of the flow of God's life.

God does not accommodate our desire to save face. He will not honor our private confession to Him because He knows our secret hearts, and He knows that we are trying to avoid the humiliation of having to confess to a brother. We would like to be alleviated of *our* distress privately, but that is contrary to the whole magnificent working of the genius of the Body of Christ. Private confession would be a deceit. We will never be willing to suffer the humiliation of confessing to a brother unless we have the deepest reverence and love for the Head of the Body. It is unbecoming to Him to have joined to that superb Head a body that is deformed, sick or disjointed, and not of the same magnificence as the Head Himself. We cannot console ourselves by saying that the sin has been met because we have confessed it to God privately; it needs first to be confessed to man. This is where the real power of it is broken and the deliverance from it comes. This is where the blood has its opportunity to be applied. This is God's biblical prescription. He knows our corrupt hearts, and knows that we can make a false piety out of this, and think that we are absolved of the thing because we have confessed it privately to Him.

Baptism and Confession

> And we refuse to bear the cross when we are
> ashamed to take upon ourselves the
> shameful death of the sinner in confession.
> In confession we break through to the true
> fellowship of the cross of Jesus Christ, in
> confession we affirm and accept our cross.
> In the deep mental and physical pain of
> humiliation before a brother - which means,
> before God - we experience the cross of
> Jesus as our rescue and salvation. The old
> man dies, but it is God who has conquered
> him. Now we share in the [reality of the]
> resurrection of Christ and eternal life.[17]

The resurrection life of God is made available in
an existential union with the crucified, resurrected One
and in fellowship with the brethren. If we are
undernourished and emaciated, it is because the life of
God has not had free course through its members. Sin
is death, and it will stop the flow and cause the
blockage of the life of God.

> In confession the breakthrough to new life
> occurs. Where sin is hated, admitted, and
> forgiven, there the break with the past is
> made...But where there is a break with sin,
> there is conversion. Confession is
> conversion.[18]

> Confession is discipleship. Life with Jesus
> Christ and his community has begun...What
> happened to us in baptism is bestowed upon
> us anew in confession.[19]

---

[17] Ibid., page 114
[18] Ibid., page 115
[19] Ibid., page 115

Confession is the one occasion given for the renewal and the release again of what baptism means, namely, death unto life.

> Why should we not find it easier to go to a brother than to the holy God?...we must ask ourselves whether we have not often been deceiving ourselves with our confession of sin to God, whether we have not rather been confessing our sins to ourselves and also granting ourselves absolution. And is not the reason perhaps for our countless relapses and the feebleness of our Christian obedience to be found precisely in the fact that we are living on self-forgiveness and not a real forgiveness? Self-forgiveness can never lead to a breach with sin; this can be accomplished only by the judging and pardoning Word of God itself.[20]

The consequences of not taking the confession of sin seriously are countless relapses and repetitions of the same sin, in the most embarrassing, least desired moment, precisely because we have been living on self-absolution and not real forgiveness.

> Who can give us the certainty that, in the confession and the forgiveness of our sins, we are not dealing with ourselves but with the living God? God gives us this certainty through our brother. Our brother breaks the circle of self-deception. A man who confesses his sins in the presence of a brother knows that he is no longer alone with himself; he experiences the presence of God in the reality of the other person...But since the sin must come to light some time,

---

[20] Ibid., pages 115-116

it is better that it happens today between me and my brother, rather than on the last day in the piercing light of the final judgment. It is a mercy that we can confess our sins to a brother. Such grace spares us the terrors of the last judgment.[21]

Though true confession is painful and humiliating, it will be much greater humiliation to experience it in the day of the Lord's judgment. Therefore, judge yourself *now* that you need not be judged *then*. For whatever remains unjudged now will come up before Him in that day.

But it is precisely for the sake of this certainty that confession should deal with *concrete* sins...Otherwise it might happen that one could still be a hypocrite even in confessing to a brother and thus miss the good of the confession.[22]

The final deception would be to go through this as a form, thinking we have the reality of it, and yet lose the benefit that God intends. Once we have given ourselves to that deception, from which deceptions are we exempt? You embrace the whole truth and nothing but the truth in order to be found walking in the truth. The truth in *this* place is the greatest assurance of truth in any other place.

In confession we, too, receive the forgiveness of the particular sins which are here brought to light, and by this very token the forgiveness of all our sins, known and unknown.[23]

---

[21] Ibid., page 116
[22] Ibid., page 117
[23] Ibid., page 117

In other words, if we are specifically identifying, clearly and truly, the sins of what we are aware, God will, at that moment, forgive our unknown sins. He waits for what we will do in truth.

To Whom do you Confess?

> To whom shall we make confession? Anybody who lives beneath the cross and who has discerned in the cross of Jesus the utter wickedness of all men and of his own heart, will find there is no sin that can ever be alien to him.[24]

You can hear the confession of another brother because *your* particular sins have been equally as abhorrent in the sight of God. The brother will not be shocked by your confession, though it may be scandalous, filthy and perverse. He knows his own heart, and if he has not been guilty of your sin, he has had one like it, or he knows that except for the grace of God, he is quite capable of exactly the same.

> Anybody who has once been horrified by the dreadfulness of his own sin that nailed Jesus to the cross will no longer be horrified by even the rankest sins of a brother. Looking at the cross of Jesus, he knows the human heart...Only the brother under the cross can hear a confession. It is not experience of life but experience of the cross that makes one a worthy hearer of confessions.[25]

---

[24] Ibid., page 118
[25] Ibid., page 118

Our qualification to receive the confession of another is that we ourselves are living in the shadow of the cross. Wonderful counseling ability and the talent to understand complex human problems disqualify us as candidates to receive confession.

> In daily, earnest living with the cross of Christ, the Christian loses the spirit of human censoriousness on the one hand and weak indulgence on the other, and he receives the spirit of divine severity and divine love.[26]

Living under the reality of the cross earnestly and consistently saves us from being judgmental and critical on the one hand where we look down our noses in contempt for the sinner who wants to confess. On the other hand, there is the weakness of being too vague, too general, too casual, where we do not see the seriousness of sin at all.

> Every person should refrain from listening to confession who does not himself practice it. Only the person who has so humbled himself can hear a brother's confession without harm.[27]

Not only does the onus rest on the person who is confessing, but just as much on the person who is hearing that confession. God puts as much requirement upon the one *hearing* the confession as on the one *making* the confession, and it is this kind of requirement that calls us to be serious before the Lord and to be walking rightly with Him.

The Lord will direct us, but let there be an amplitude of candidates in every fellowship who live in the shadow of the cross, who can be ones to whom

---

[26] Ibid., page 119
[27] Ibid., page 120

we can confess. In most cases, it is hard to find even one. In other words, it is not safe to confess, except to a man who humbles himself and suffers the indignity and the humiliation of confessing to others himself. Look for someone who you can have access to on a frequent if not daily basis. Do not seek for someone who will be sympathetic with your carnal flesh.

> The second danger concerns the confessant [the one who is confessing]. For the salvation of his soul, let him guard against ever making a pious work of his confession. If he does so, it will become the final, most abominable, vicious, and impure prostitution of the heart; the act becomes an idle, lustful babbling. Confession as a pious work is an invention of the devil.[28]

We can trivialize the things that are holy, and there is nothing more deceitful than a false confession. We would be better off not having ever made it than to make it and make it insincerely. We give the sin a greater power for a more absolute domination over us by a phony attempt that never intended to see its power broken. Confession of one's sins is a sacred, precious and holy act of obedience, and the integrity of it needs to be maintained. Confession should never be set up in a religious way. Rather, the quality, or the character of our corporate life should make plenty of room for it.

---

[28] Ibid., page 120

Chapter 12

Communion: The Joyful Sacrament

> And when He [Jesus] had taken some bread
> and given thanks, He broke it and gave it to
> them, saying, "This is My body which is
> given for you; do this in remembrance of
> Me."
> And in the same way He took the cup after
> they had eaten, saying, "This cup which is
> poured out for you is the new covenant in My
> blood."[1]

As a young, Pentecostal believer, the taking of
communion, also known as the Lord's Supper, was an
agonizing experience. I dreaded that once-a-month
occasion when the plastic cups were circulated,
intuiting that something was not right. The anonymity
of it was so abstract and antiseptic; it was not life-
giving at all. I did not even *want* to take it. We were

---

[1] Luke 22:19-20

taking communion without confession, and taking the holy blood of the Lamb, not discerning the Body of Christ, not even discerning the blood, and washing it down as if it were soda pop. We were living in unconfessed and murky sins, and taking communion with those who were strangers rather than with brothers to whom we could have confessed our sins. It was a mock, and we were losing the efficacy of the spiritual reality that inheres in both the bread and the wine. We were taking communion as a religious ceremony, a biblical requirement, and were therefore losing the very thing for which it was given, namely, to maintain the life and virility of the fellowship.

Bonhoeffer continues in his book, *Life Together*:

> The day of the Lord's Supper is an occasion of joy for the Christian community. Reconciled in their hearts with God and the brethren, the congregation receives the gift of the Body and blood of Jesus Christ, and, receiving that, it receives forgiveness, new life, and salvation.[2]

The sacraments of God are holy and divinely inspired; they are also life-giving, spiritual realities. In modern times, the sacrament of communion has become a practice that does not seem to confer what Bonhoeffer is suggesting, namely, forgiveness, new life and salvation. One of the key reasons for this is that we have separated confession from communion. The confession of sin, the clearing of the air and the reconciling of broken relationships must necessarily precede communion, otherwise we make communion a lie.

In the traditional Catholic understanding, the taking of communion is called the Eucharist, in which

_____
[2] page 122

the bread and wine are believed to magically become the literal and actual body and blood of the Lord Himself. It is their doctrine of transubstantiation, and is erroneous, in my opinion. But the Protestant side has moved to an error of an equal and comparable kind by describing the Eucharist language of bread and wine as mere emblems or symbols. In other words, by being merely symbolic or representative, they have a lesser significance, and are something we are required to observe as a remembrance only.

My own feeling is in agreement with Bonhoeffer, that the receiving of communion after confession actually ministers new life and salvation to the Body of Christ. The grace of God and the power of His life flow again to break the power of sin, cleanse the soul and revive the spirit. The bread and the wine do not have magical powers in and of themselves, but rather the reality behind the elements confers the continuing ministry of renewal by the Holy Spirit into the divine image. Do we have the faith to appropriate this blessed promise and provision? On what basis are we presently seeking the renewing of His life and salvation?

> While they were eating, Jesus took some bread, and after a blessing, He broke it and gave it to the disciples, and said, "Take, eat; this is My body." And when He had taken a cup and given thanks, He gave it to them, saying, "Drink from it, all of you; for this is My blood of the covenant, which is poured out for many for forgiveness of sins. But I say to you, I will not drink of this fruit of the vine from now on until that day when I

drink it new with you in My Father's kingdom."[3]

In his book on spiritual realities, Watchman Nee wrote:

> Note that Jesus said, "This is My body" rather than, "This represents My body." And after He said, "This is My blood of the covenant," the Lord continued with, "I will not drink of this fruit of the vine from now on," clearly indicating that the wine had neither been transubstantiated nor is representative of the blood.[4]

In other words, Jesus laid emphasis neither on transubstantiation nor on representation but on spiritual reality, and that behind what is eaten and drunk is the spiritual reality. "Is not the cup of blessing which we bless a sharing in the blood of Christ? Is not the bread which we break a sharing in the body of Christ?"[5] Nee goes on to write:

> Here is one [Paul] who really knows the Lord. When he takes up the bread he is truly in communion with the body of Christ, for he has forgotten the bread and is now in touch with the spiritual reality. When he takes the cup he is indeed in communion with the blood of Christ, for he has forgotten the fruit of the vine and has touched the spiritual reality.[6]

Communion is one of God's precious and gracious provisions, none of which would be life-giving if there

---

[3] Matthew 26:26-29

[4] *Spiritual Reality or Obsession* by Watchman Nee, page 9, © 1970 Christian Fellowship Publishers, Inc.

[5] 1 Corinthians 10:16

[6] *Spiritual Reality or Obsession*, page 10

were not a death and resurrection, a body that was broken, and blood that was shed. It will only become a blessing for us when it is sacred, when it is holy, when it is true, when it is righteous, and when it is done in love. God forbid that we should limp along, and not have what God has given us as a precious grace for the ongoing life of God in our daily walk in fellowship with the Body. The taking of communion is not a little addendum to our predictable Christianity, but it will remain so until we have been apprehended by the reality of it in the context of the Body of Christ.

A Life-Giving Sacrament

> So Jesus said to them, "Truly, truly, I say to you, unless you eat the flesh of the Son of Man and drink His blood, you have no life in yourselves. He who eats My flesh and drinks My blood has eternal life, and I will raise him up on the last day. For My flesh is true food, and My blood is true drink. He who eats My flesh and drinks My blood abides in Me, and I in Him. As the living Father sent Me, and I live because of the Father, so he who eats Me, he also will live because of Me. This is the bread which came down out of heaven; not as the fathers ate, and died; he who eats this bread will live forever."[7]

The passage goes on to say that through lack of faith many of His disciples withdrew, and did not walk with Him anymore.[8] Unbelief, the unwillingness to appropriate by faith the spiritual and eternal content of

---

[7] John 6:53-58
[8] Ibid., see v.66

the word of God, will always lead to a pulling away from God. The sacrament of communion becomes a sacrament that is life-giving when we are actually eating and drinking *of Him*; it is to draw our life sustenance from Him; but there first needs to be a recognition of the need for that drawing. This can only grow out of the awareness of how much is required to be in authentic fellowship with the brethren on a daily basis. Only then will we find that we need the life of God, the strength of God and the compassion of God; we will need to eat and drink of Him.

No more can we allow the taking of communion to degenerate into a religious practice, taken mindlessly, in which the entire value is lost. If it is not taken on the basis of faith and truth, that which is intended as life will become death. In other words, those who do not receive it as life, will receive it as death, and for that reason many are weak, sick and some die.[9]

> The fellowship of the Lord's Supper is the superlative fulfillment of Christian fellowship. As the members of the congregation are united in body and blood at the table of the Lord so will they be together in eternity. Here the community has reached its goal. Here joy in Christ and His community is complete. The life of Christians together under the Word has reached its perfection in the sacrament.[10]

Bonhoeffer saw this practice established in time as being already a foretaste of that fellowship which is everlasting. Only then can those who are sent from us move in the life and the power of that sending

---

[9] See 1 Corinthians 11:30
[10] *Life Together*, page 122

fellowship. It is reality, life and power because the conditions for it have been obtained and maintained. We are eating and drinking of the body of the Lord; it is a foretaste of heaven; it is the perfection and completion of the whole purpose for which we have our being.

How to Minister the Sacrament

Our true fellowship may not necessarily be in a regular church situation but in a small handful of believers in a living room. It is with these that we share our life; it is with these that we confess ours sins; it is with these that we walk in truth, and it is with these that we can therefore receive the grace that God gives when communion is taken in truth and by faith.

When you are the one ministering the sacrament, your responsibility is to guard the holiness of the communion table, and not to make it a cheap practice by those who are undiscerning and mindless, and who are just going through the mechanics of it. You may have to find yourself announcing, "I have this responsibility. You are welcome to the table as a believer in communion with Christ. I need to remind those who are believers, but who are living in unconfessed sin, that according to the scriptures, you will be drinking to your own judgment. You will experience this as sickness and perhaps as death, and I would encourage you not to take it without first making right what needs to be made right. I am not at liberty to serve those of you who are not believers. I hope you will not be offended, but you have to understand that I have an obligation before God to keep the sanctity of this table."

With regard to children, the Lord is gracious, and understands that there is no wicked intention or motive, and that the children, in their innocence, want to participate with their parents. They can take it even though they are not of an age in which the parents can explain the conditions for communion. What they receive the Lord knows, but He is not likely to be offended.

A Final Word

We should never allow the Lord's Supper to become a methodology, but rather an environment in which the sense of the holiness of God prevails. It is a renewing of the covenant, and we are eating and drinking the Lord afresh. We are showing again that we are cast upon His life. Our coming to the communion table is a statement that we are not only in union with God in authenticity in the sacrificial giving up of ourselves, but also with the brethren at large. We are giving our life up. We would enjoy our privacy, but the demands of the Body of Christ require our participation, and we give ourselves in communion with them.

May we be found esteeming the blood of Jesus, and take the cup in sincerity and truth, thus avoiding a sleep that may end in death. May we have the desire to see our fellowship abound in vitality and power; may we experience the flow of the resurrection life in the fulfillment of the purposes that can only come by it, *through* the Body. May we ask the Lord to show us the pride and privatistic hiding that exists in each one of us, and give us a desire to search our own hearts, rather than wait to be scandalously exposed and caught in our sin. Let us be clean and stay clean, which we cannot do or maintain by *ourselves*; it requires the operation of the Body, and we need to be in an expression of the Body where these realities are foundational and operating daily. There is no power or authority given by God to deal with the powers of the air outside of this reality made available only in the Body.

It was only when Jesus broke the bread and gave the blessing at the communion table that the disciples' eyes were open, and they recognized who He was. May our eyes be opened every time the bread is broken in truth. Communion without the sense of the holiness of God is not communion. The very environment, the sense of the holiness of it, will affect the people to respond accordingly. And that environment is the environment of truth, light, love and righteousness. In that kind of environment, we will receive the full benefit of God's intention. This is a glimpse of what church means in truth if it is to be for God a glory, not only in this age, but also in the ages to come. What an attention it requires, and what a devotion and a jealousy! What a demand upon our time!

May the Lord grant an increasing desire for communion again. May it be taken authentically, in faith, with love unfeigned, with those with whom we are sharing a common life. May we receive the full value of God's life and provision. Bonhoeffer received his insights in a time of suffering. May these realities serve us as a precious last days' provision enabling us to stand firm in an inevitable, soon-coming time when we will be facing the same pressures that Bonhoeffer did. Amen.

OTHER BOOKS by Art Katz

REALITY: THE HOPE OF GLORY

The four messages in this book are a powerful inspiration to those who will not settle for less than the true meaning of life as a disciple of Christ. Paperback, 156 pages.

THE SPIRIT OF TRUTH

Into this age of religious pretension, exaggeration and deception, Art brings a deep, incisive probing into the nature of truth. Every lover and guardian of truth will find this an insightful and demanding book. Paperback, 101 pages.

APOSTOLIC FOUNDATIONS

In his penetrating manner, Art shows that a church with apostolic foundations is a body of people whose central impulse is a radical and total jealousy for the glory of God. It was so at the church's inception, and needs to be so at its conclusion. Paperback, 272 pages.

BEN ISRAEL – ODYSSEY OF A MODERN JEW

Written as a literal journal, Art recounts his experience as an atheist and former Marxist being apprehended by a God whom he was not seeking. The message of this book has been powerfully used to bring other of Art's Jewish kinsmen to the faith of their fathers. Paperback, 149 pages.

THE HOLOCAUST: WHERE WAS GOD? – *An inquiry into the biblical roots of tragedy.*

In a daring hypothesis, the author turns to the ancient Hebrew scriptures as the key of interpretation to one of the most catastrophic events of modern times: the Jewish Holocaust of World War II. In this examination of that ultimate tragedy, the issue of God *as God* is brought courageously to the forefront of our modern consideration as few books have attempted to do. Paperback, 91 pages.

THE TEMPTATIONS OF CHRIST – A CALL TO SONSHIP AND MATURITY

The scriptures indicate that Jesus was led into the wilderness in the *fullness* of the Spirit, but came out of that testing place in the *power* of the Spirit. The author examines the necessary progression in our Christian lives without which we will never be able to convey the knowledge of the risen Christ. Paperback, 56 pages.

WHAT A JEW DOES WITH JESUS

Despite the apparent contradiction, the author pleads with his Jewish kinsmen to take into their deepest consideration the truth that biblical Judaism is determined solely by what we do with Jesus of Nazareth. Paperback, 128 pages.

THE ANATOMY OF DECEPTION

In a dark and seductive age, and one that is increasingly abounding in deception and lying signs, the ability to discern between the false and the true is of paramount importance. Paperback, 60 pages.